THE PRO WRESTLING LAWS OF SUCCESS

ALSO BY DONNIE HOOVER

The Pro Wrestling Laws of Success
Know Yourself, Master the 10 Laws, Build an Unbreakable Mindset

UPCOMING RELEASES

The Pro Wrestling Laws of Business
Read People, Make Money, Build a Legacy That Outlasts Your Career

The Pro Wrestling Laws of AI
How to Use Technology to Dominate Your Career and Your Income

The Pro Wrestling Laws of Promotion
How to Run a Wrestling Company, Fill Seats, and Build an Empire

THE PRO WRESTLING LAWS OF SUCCESS

Know Yourself, Master the 10 Laws,
Build an Unbreakable Mindset

Book One of The Pro Wrestling Laws Trilogy

DONNIE HOOVER

Hoover Publishing, LLC

The Pro Wrestling Laws of Success

Know Yourself, Master the 10 Laws, Build an Unbreakable Mindset

Published by Hoover Publishing
www.prowrestlingskool.com

Book One of The Pro Wrestling Laws Trilogy

First Edition: 2026
ISBN: [978-0-9830677-3-3]
eBook ISBN: [978-0-9830677-2-6]

Printed in the United States of America

For booking, speaking engagements, or bulk orders:
www.ProWrestlingSkool.com

For Terrie.

You believed in every crazy idea I ever had.
You stood next to me when the bank account said quit.
You let me come back to wrestling when most wives would have said no.
None of this exists without you.

And for every wrestler who was told they'd never make it.
Keep going.

CONTENTS

THE TRILOGY AT A GLANCE

Book 1: The Pro Wrestling Laws of Success
The Mind. How to think.

Book 2: The Pro Wrestling Laws of Business
The Money. How to build.

Book 3: The Pro Wrestling Laws of AI
The Machine. How to accelerate.

The 3R Framework drives everything:
Reach. Reputation. Revenue.

This is Book One. The foundation.
Everything starts here.

HOW THIS BOOK IS ORGANIZED

This book is built in two parts. Each part builds on the one before it. But you can also jump to whatever section you need most right now.

Part One: Know Yourself

Before you can succeed, you have to understand who you are. Your strengths. Your weaknesses. Your personality type. Your blind spots. This section helps you figure out what kind of wrestler you really are and why that self-knowledge is the foundation of everything else.

Part Two: Pro Wrestling Laws of Success

These are the ten principles that separate winners from everyone else in this business. Mindset. Belief. Skill. Imagination. Planning. Decision-making. Persistence. Teamwork. Emotional control. Mental programming. Master these laws and you'll outperform wrestlers with twice your talent.

What Comes Next: Book Two, Pro Wrestling Laws of Business

The Laws of Success are just the beginning. In Pro Wrestling Laws of Business, you'll learn how to read people, build a real business, and create a legacy that outlasts your in-ring career. Reading promoters. Working crowds. Making money multiple ways. Building your brand. Creating digital income. Long-term wealth and freedom. The Laws of Success give you the engine. Pro Wrestling Laws of Business shows you where to drive it.

Your Free Bonus: Join Pro Wrestling Skool

At the end of this book, you'll find an invitation to join the free Pro Wrestling Skool community. Inside, you'll get access to the tools that go with this book: the 3R Framework on one page, a 30-day mindset challenge, weekly planning templates, a gimmick development worksheet, a content calendar, and a growing library of resources to keep you moving forward. The book gives you the laws. The community gives you the tools to put them to work.

A Note Before You Start

You don't have to read this book in order.

If you're struggling with confidence, jump to Chapter 4.

But eventually, read the whole thing. The pieces connect. The laws reinforce each other. The full picture is more powerful than any single chapter.

Now turn the page and let's get to work.

INTRODUCTION
WHY WRESTLERS WIN

You're broke.

You love wrestling more than anything else in your life. You think about it when you wake up. You think about it at your day job. You think about it when you're lying in bed at night staring at the ceiling.

But your bank account doesn't care how much you love it.

You're driving three hours to wrestle for gas money or a hot dog and handshake. You're posting on Instagram and getting 12 likes. You're watching other wrestlers blow up online while you're stuck in the same spot you were in two years ago.

You keep telling yourself it'll get better. You keep waiting for your big break. You keep hoping some promoter will notice you and change your life.

But nothing's changing.

You're tired. You're frustrated. And somewhere deep down, in a place you don't like to visit, you're starting to wonder if this whole thing was a mistake.

I know that feeling. I've lived in that place.

And I'm going to show you how to get out.

Who I Am

My name is Donnie Hoover.

I'm a semi-retired professional wrestler. I'm a promoter. I'm a trainer. I'm a gym owner. I'm building an online education platform for wrestlers. And I've been in and around this business since 1997.

That's almost 30 years of bumps, lessons, failures, and wins.

I've wrestled in front of crowds that were on fire. I've wrestled in front of crowds that sat on their hands like they were waiting for a bus. I've worked with pro wrestling legends. I've worked with guys who went on to make it big. I've worked with guys who quit and never came back.

I've driven multiple hours for a show that got canceled when I pulled into the parking lot.

I've been stiffed by promoters. I've been promised things that never happened. I've been told I was going to be a star by people who forgot my name a week later.

I've also built something real.

Today my wife Terrie and I run New Ohio Wrestling, a live family-friendly wrestling promotion. I own the NOW Elite Pro Wrestling Academy where I train the next generation of pro wrestlers in partnership with "Superman" Onyx. And Terrie and I operate the WrestleFit Training & Lifestyle Center, a functional fitness gym built on pro wrestling training principles, with "Superman" Onyx as our partner and head trainer. I also created Pro Wrestling Skool, an online platform teaching wrestlers worldwide how to build brands, grow audiences, and make real money.

At the time I'm writing this book, New Ohio Wrestling is the only independent pro wrestling company in the world to ever perform at the Arnold Sports Festival. Not just once. We've been there multiple times. We've run shows on one of the biggest stages in the fitness and sports world. And during one of our championship matches, Arnold Schwarzenegger himself came down to ringside and got involved in the action.

Read that again.

Arnold Schwarzenegger. The Terminator. The Oak. One of the most famous human beings on the planet. Standing at ringside during a New Ohio Wrestling match.

I'm not saying that to brag. I'm saying it because I need you to understand something. You can build something from nothing.

You can take an indie wrestling promotion that nobody's heard of and put it in places nobody thought possible. You can create moments that seem impossible until you make them happen.

If I can get Arnold Schwarzenegger to ringside, you can figure out how to get more bookings and make more money.

I'm not rich. I'm not famous. I'm not on TV.

But I'm building something that's mine. Something nobody can take from me. Something that will outlast my body's ability to take bumps.

And I want to show you how to do the same thing.

The Day I Walked Away

In 2002, I had to make the hardest decision of my life.

My body wasn't just breaking down. It was falling apart.

Six concussions. A brain bleed that almost killed me. A broken nose. A dislocated wrist. Multiple scars from hardcore matches. I'd lost more blood than I want to think about. I was hurting in places I didn't know could hurt. And the injuries weren't just adding up. They were compounding.

Every time I stepped in the ring, I was rolling the dice with my life.

And my wife Terrie and I were struggling financially. We were starting a family. We had real responsibilities. Real bills. Real pressure. I couldn't keep destroying my body for $20 paydays and broken promises.

I looked at wrestling. I looked at my life. And I realized I couldn't do both.

Not the way I was doing it.

So I walked away.

I want you to understand what that felt like. Wrestling wasn't just something I did. It was who I was. It was my identity. It was the thing that made me feel alive.

Walking away from it felt like cutting off a part of myself.

But I had to survive. I had a wife who believed in me. I had a family counting on me. And I couldn't keep chasing a dream that was breaking my body and draining my bank account.

So I stepped out of the ring. I got a regular job. I did what I had to do.

But I never stopped watching. I never stopped studying. I never stopped loving this business.

For over a decade, I kept my finger on the pulse of pro wrestling. I watched who was making money. I studied what was working. I paid attention to the business side of things in a way I never had when I was active.

And I waited.

The Comeback

By 2014, things had changed.

Terrie and I had built a stable life. Our family was in a good place. We had financial breathing room for the first time in years. And that itch, that pull toward wrestling, it never went away. It just got louder.

I talked to Terrie about it. Really talked. Not the kind of conversation where you're trying to convince someone. The kind where you're honest about what you want and what it might cost.

She understood. She always has.

In 2015, we made the decision together. We started New Ohio Wrestling.

It wasn't a big deal at first. Just a small promotion. Local shows. Building something from nothing. But it was ours. And it was real.

That was the beginning of everything.

In 2021, right after COVID turned the world upside down, I opened the WrestleFit Training & Lifestyle Center with Terrie and our partner "Superman" Onyx. A gym built on the training methods we'd learned from wrestling. Functional fitness. Real strength. The kind of training that actually prepares your body for life.

In 2024, I launched the NOW Elite Pro Wrestling Academy in partnership with "Superman" Onyx. A real wrestling school where we could pass on everything we'd learned to the next generation.

And in 2025, I started building Pro Wrestling Skool. An online platform where pro wrestlers anywhere in the world could learn the business side of this industry. The stuff nobody teaches you. The stuff I had to figure out the hard way. And still am.

The Truth Nobody Tells You

I need you to understand something.

I still have a day job.

That might surprise you. You might be reading this thinking I'm some success story who figured it all out and now I'm living the dream full time.

Not yet.

My day job pays well. It gives me the financial foundation to run these businesses without desperation. It lets me build things the right way instead of cutting corners because I need cash this week.

But it's not where I want to be forever.

I'm telling you this because I want you to know I'm not some guru on a mountaintop pretending I have all the answers. I'm in the trenches with you. I'm building this thing in real time. I'm figuring it out as I go.

The difference is I have a system. I have a plan. I have a framework that's working.

And I want to share all of it with you.

Pro Wrestling Skool isn't just me teaching you what I learned in the past. It's me bringing you along as I build toward freedom right now. You're going to learn everything I'm learning. You're going to see what works and what doesn't. You're going to watch me make mistakes and figure out solutions.

We're doing this together.

The Problem With Wrestling

So why do wrestlers stay broke?

It's not because they're not talented. There are thousands of incredibly talented wrestlers out there working for gas money. Talent isn't the problem.

It's not because they don't work hard. Wrestlers are some of the hardest working people on the planet. You don't survive in this business without a serious work ethic.

It's not because they don't love it enough. Wrestlers love this business so much it hurts. That's actually part of the problem.

The reason wrestlers stay broke is simple.

Nobody taught them how to make money.

What does wrestling school teach you? How to take a bump. How to run the ropes. How to work a match. How to sell. How to cut a promo.

All of that is important. You can't be a wrestler without it.

But what doesn't wrestling school teach you?

How to build a brand. How to grow an audience. How to get booked consistently. How to negotiate your pay. How to create multiple income streams. How to make money online. How to build something that pays you even when you're not in the ring.

You're expected to figure all of that out on your own.

And most wrestlers never do.

They think if they just get better in the ring, the money will follow. If they just work harder, someone will notice. If they just keep showing up, their big break will come.

That's a lie.

Being good in the ring is the bare minimum. It's the entry fee. It's what gets you in the door. But it's not what makes you money.

You need more than moves. You need a system.

The 3R Framework

This book teaches you a system. I call it the 3R Framework.

It's built on three pillars.

Reach. This is your audience. Your visibility. How many people know you exist.

A lot of wrestlers think they need to be on TV to have reach. That's old thinking. You can build reach right now with your phone. YouTube. Instagram. TikTok. Facebook. You can reach thousands of people without asking a single promoter for permission.

Reach is how you stop being invisible.

Reputation. This is how people see you. Your brand. Your character. Your reliability. Your professionalism.

Promoters book wrestlers they trust. Fans follow wrestlers they believe in. Your reputation is the invisible force that opens doors or keeps them closed.

If you show up on time, work safe, put on great matches, and handle yourself like a professional, your reputation grows. Word spreads. Opportunities appear.

If you're late, sloppy, difficult, or unreliable, your reputation dies. And it dies faster than you think.

Reputation is how you become undeniable.

Revenue. This is money. Income. Wealth. The actual financial reward for everything you do.

Right now, you probably make money one way. Bookings. You work a show, you get paid, you go home. If you don't work, you don't get paid.

That's a trap.

If you get hurt, your income stops. If you get blackballed by a promoter, your income stops. If bookings dry up, your income stops. You're one bad break away from nothing.

You need multiple streams of income. In-ring money from bookings. Online money from content, courses, and communities. Passive money from digital products and affiliate deals. Merch money. Appearance money. Coaching money.

Revenue is how you get free.

Reach. Reputation. Revenue. The 3R Framework.

It's simple. It's practical. And it works.

Why Wrestlers Are Built for This

Something most people miss about wrestlers.

You already have the skills to succeed in business. You just don't know it yet.

Look at what you do every time you step in the ring.

You perform under pressure. Live. In front of a crowd. No second takes. No do-overs. No safety net. You have to deliver right now or you fail in front of everyone.

Most people are terrified of that. You do it for fun.

You read people. You can feel a crowd's energy and adjust on the fly. You know when they're with you and when you're losing them. You make real-time decisions based on feedback most people can't even perceive.

That's a superpower.

You handle rejection. You've been told no more times than you can count. You've had bad matches. You've had crowds that didn't care. You've been passed over for opportunities you deserved. And you kept going anyway.

That mental toughness is rare.

You create from nothing. You build characters. You develop storylines. You create personas that connect with people emotionally. You're a writer, an actor, and a performer all in one.

That's creative firepower most people don't have.

You sell yourself. Every time you step in the ring, you're convincing a crowd to care about you. Every promo is a sales pitch. Every match is a demonstration of value. You've been marketing yourself your whole career.

You just didn't call it marketing.

These skills transfer directly to business. Performance under pressure. Reading people. Mental toughness. Creativity. Self-promotion.

That's the exact toolkit you need to build a brand, grow an audience, and make money online.

You're not starting from zero. You're starting with advantages most people would kill for.

This book shows you how to use them.

What This Book Will Do for You

This is not a book about wrestling moves. You already know how to wrestle. Or you're learning.

This is a book about the mental game. The business game. The long-term game.

By the time you finish this book, you'll understand:

How to think like the wrestlers who actually make it.

How to build a character that fans invest in emotionally.

How to get booked more often and paid more money.

Every chapter gives you a law. A principle. A tool you can use immediately.

Who This Book Is For

This book is for indie wrestlers who want to stand out in a crowded market.

It's for wrestlers who want more bookings and better pay.

It's for wrestlers who want to make real money, not just gas money.

It's for trainers who want to build their academies into real businesses.

It's for promoters who want to grow their promotions and increase their profits.

It's for referees, managers, valets, and ring crew who want to turn their roles into something bigger.

It's for hardcore fans who want to understand the game behind the game.

If you're serious about wrestling as a career, this book is for you.

If you're just doing this for fun and you never plan to make a dime, this book is still for you. Because the lessons in here apply to everything. Business. Relationships. Life. The principles work whether you're trying to get booked or trying to get promoted at your day job.

How to Use This Book

Read it once all the way through. Get the big picture. Let the ideas sink in.

Then go back and work through the exercises. Every chapter has action steps. Do them. Don't just read about success. Practice it.

Take notes. Highlight things. Write in the margins. Dog-ear the pages.

This isn't a book you read once and put on a shelf to impress people. This is a playbook. A manual. A system.

Use it.

My Promise to You

I'm not going to lie to you in this book.

I'm not going to hype you up with fake guru energy and empty promises.

I'm not going to tell you that you'll be a millionaire in six months if you just follow my secret formula.

There is no secret formula. There's just work. Smart work. Consistent work. Work that compounds over time into something real.

What I will tell you is this.

If you apply the laws in this book, you will get better results than you're getting now. You will get more bookings. You will make more money. You will build something that lasts.

But you have to do the work.

Nobody is coming to save you. No promoter is going to discover you and make you a star. No viral video is going to change your life overnight. No lucky break is going to fix your problems.

You have to build it yourself. Brick by brick. Day by day. Post by post. Match by match.

This book shows you how.

Let's Go

The wrestler who wins is the one who never stops learning.

You're here. You're reading this. You invested in yourself. That already puts you ahead of most people in the locker room who think they know everything and refuse to grow.

You're different.

Now let's prove it.

Your next 90 days start right now. Not tomorrow. Not next week. Not when the timing is perfect.

Now.

Turn the page. Let's get to work.

— Donnie Hoover

PART ONE
KNOW YOURSELF

CHAPTER 1
WHAT KIND OF WRESTLER ARE YOU?

Two wrestlers walk into a training school on the same day.

Same trainer. Same drills. Same bumps. Same bruises.

Three years later, one of them is getting booked every weekend, building a fanbase, making real money. The other quit wrestling and works at a warehouse. Bitter. Broken. Wondering what went wrong.

What happened?

The one who succeeded figured out who he really was. The one who quit kept trying to be someone else.

This is the mistake that kills more pro wrestling careers than injuries, politics, or bad luck combined. Wrestlers spend years trying to be the next somebody instead of becoming the first them.

They copy their favorite wrestlers move for move. They do whatever their trainer tells them without question. They chase gimmicks that don't fit their personality. They force characters that feel fake the moment they open their mouth.

And they wonder why crowds don't connect with them.

The answer is simple. You can't build a career on someone else's personality. You can't get over pretending to be something you're not. Crowds smell fake from a mile away.

You have to know yourself first.

Your strengths. Your weaknesses. Your natural style. The thing that makes you different from every other wrestler on the card.

This chapter helps you figure that out.

The Question Nobody Asks

This might surprise you.

Most wrestlers have never sat down and seriously asked themselves what kind of wrestler they are. They've thought about what moves they want to do. They've thought about what gimmick sounds cool. They've thought about who they want to be like.

But they've never done the deeper work of figuring out who they actually are.

This is a problem.

Because everything in your career flows from that answer. Your character. Your moveset. Your promos. Your brand. Your content. The promoters you work best with. The opponents you have chemistry with. The fans who will become your loyal followers.

All of it starts with knowing yourself.

If you get this wrong, you'll spend years swimming upstream. Forcing things that don't fit. Burning out because you're playing a character that exhausts you. Wondering why other wrestlers are passing you by.

If you get this right, everything gets easier. Your character feels natural. Your promos flow without scripting every word. Crowds respond because they sense something real. Promoters book you because you're easy to work with and consistent.

Self-knowledge is the foundation. Everything else is built on top of it.

The 9 Wrestler Personality Types

Every wrestler fits into one of nine core personality types.

This isn't astrology. This isn't some made-up nonsense to sell you a quiz. This is based on observing hundreds of wrestlers over decades and noticing patterns in who succeeds and why.

Each type has natural strengths. Things that come easy to them. Things they can lean into and dominate with.

Each type has natural weaknesses. Blind spots. Areas where they'll struggle if they don't get help or put in extra work.

Each type fits certain gimmicks better than others. When your character matches your type, magic happens. When it doesn't, everything feels forced.

Your job right now is to figure out which type you are. Be honest with yourself. Don't pick the type you wish you were. Pick the type you actually are.

Here are the nine types.

Type 1: The Powerhouse

These are the wrestlers who own the room the moment they walk in.

Big. Strong. Physical. Dominant presence. They don't have to say a word. Their size and energy do the talking. People respect them immediately because their body commands respect.

Powerhouses are natural at physicality. Power moves. Big slams. Impact spots that make crowds gasp. They're believable winners. When a Powerhouse beats someone, it makes sense. Nobody questions it.

They're also natural leaders. Other wrestlers look to them for guidance. They set the tone in the locker room. They become the anchor that younger wrestlers rally around.

But Powerhouses have blind spots.

They're not always great talkers. They can rely too much on their size instead of developing real character depth. Promoters might typecast them as monsters or enforcers when they're capable of more. And as they age, their body becomes harder to maintain.

The best gimmicks for Powerhouses are dominant characters. Monster heels. Unstoppable champions. Enforcers. Bodyguards. Authority figures. Silent destroyers who let their actions speak.

If you're a Powerhouse, your presence is your money. Don't fight it. Don't try to be a comedy guy or a high-flyer. Be the immovable object. Be the guy everyone else has to survive.

Type 2: The Performer

Born for the spotlight. That's the Performer.

Charismatic. Entertaining. Magnetic. They light up when the crowd is watching. They feed off the energy and give it back tenfold. They understand timing, rhythm, and drama instinctively.

Performers connect with crowds instantly. They're great on the mic. They know how to work a room. They turn average matches into memorable moments through sheer force of personality.

They're natural storytellers. Every match has a beginning, middle, and end. Every promo has a hook. They make people feel something.

The flip side?

They can prioritize entertainment over in-ring fundamentals. They might overdo it and come off as trying too hard. They need constant validation from the crowd, which can mess with their head on quiet nights. And they sometimes struggle with consistency because they're always chasing the next big reaction.

Gimmicks that work for Performers: Showmen. Egomaniacs. Charismatic leaders. Comedy characters with depth. Larger-than-life personalities that fill the arena.

If you're a Performer, entertainment is your weapon. Don't let anyone tell you to tone it down. Focus on promos, character work, and crowd interaction. That's where you'll separate yourself from everyone else.

Type 3: The Technician

If wrestling is a craft, Technicians are the master builders.

Detail-oriented. Skilled. Precise. They care about doing things right. Their moves are clean. Their timing is sharp. They make their opponents look good because they understand the mechanics of what makes wrestling work.

Technicians are the backbone of any roster. They can work with anyone. They elevate green wrestlers. They have safe, crisp matches that promoters trust. They're students of the game who never stop learning.

They earn respect through competence. Other wrestlers want to work with them because they know the match will be good. Trainers trust them to help break in new talent.

Where Technicians struggle is connection.

They can get so focused on the technical side that they forget to connect emotionally. They might have perfect matches that crowds don't care about because there's no story. They can be overlooked for flashier wrestlers who aren't as skilled but have more charisma. And they sometimes struggle with promos because talking feels less natural than wrestling.

Characters that fit Technicians: Submission specialists. Mat wrestlers. Coaches. Veterans. No-nonsense competitors who let their work speak for itself.

If you're a Technician, your craft is your calling card. Don't try to be something you're not. Focus on being the best worker on the card. Build your reputation on reliability and skill. That's a career that lasts.

Type 4: The Thinker

While everyone else is focused on the next match, the Thinker is planning the next year.

Strategic. Analytical. Always planning three moves ahead. They understand wrestling as a business, not just a performance. They think about booking, storylines, and long-term career positioning.

Thinkers are valuable because they bring more than just wrestling ability. They can help book shows. They can structure storylines. They can see what's missing from a card and fill the gap. They're natural promoters and bookers even if they never officially take those roles.

They're also great at managing their own careers. They make smart decisions about who to work with, what gimmicks to pursue, and when to make moves. They don't just react to opportunities. They create them.

The downside of all that brainpower?

They can overthink everything and lose spontaneity. They might come across as cold or calculated when crowds want raw emotion. They can get frustrated when promoters don't see what they see. And they sometimes struggle to turn off the analytical brain and just perform in the moment.

Thinkers thrive as masterminds. Managers. Authority figures. Calculating heels who outsmart their opponents. Chess players in a checkers world.

If you're a Thinker, your brain is your advantage. Use it. But don't let it paralyze you. Learn to balance strategy with spontaneity. Your path might lead to promoting, training, or booking as much as performing.

Type 5: The Fighter

Pure intensity. That's what Fighters run on.

Emotional. Passionate. Driven by fire. They wrestle like every match is life or death. They bring an energy that's impossible to fake. When they're in the ring, you believe they want to win more than anything.

Fighters connect with crowds through raw emotion. They're natural underdogs because people root for passion. They're also natural heels because that same intensity can turn dark and dangerous.

They don't hold back. They leave everything in the ring. They have the kind of matches that people remember years later because the emotion was so real.

That fire comes with a cost.

They can burn too hot and flame out. They might struggle to pace themselves over a long career. They can let emotions override smart decisions. And they sometimes have trouble with the business side because they care more about the fight than the money.

Fighters shine brightest as underdogs. Brawlers. Anti-heroes. Passionate babyfaces who never quit. Dangerous heels who've snapped.

If you're a Fighter, your fire is your gift. Don't let anyone dim it. But learn to control it. Channel that intensity into sustainable fuel, not explosive burnout.

Type 6: The Daredevil

Every crowd has that moment where everyone holds their breath. Daredevils live for that moment.

Athletic. Fearless. Willing to take risks that other wrestlers won't. They fly through the air. They attempt moves that seem impossible. They put their bodies on the line for moments that make people jump out of their seats.

Daredevils create highlight reels. They're the wrestlers whose clips go viral. They bring an excitement to shows that no other type can match. When a Daredevil is on the card, fans know they're going to see something special.

They're also incredibly athletic. Their bodies can do things that most people can't comprehend. They've trained their coordination, timing, and spatial awareness to superhuman levels.

The price of fearlessness is steep.

Their style is brutal on the body. Injuries are common. Careers can be short. They can become addicted to the pop and keep escalating risks until something breaks. They might struggle to adapt when their body slows down. And they can be one-dimensional if they don't develop character and promo skills to go with the athleticism.

Daredevils get the biggest reactions as high-flyers. Luchadors. Stunt performers. Adrenaline junkies. The wrestler who does things nobody else will try.

If you're a Daredevil, your fearlessness is your edge. But protect your body. Learn to get reactions without always going to the biggest spot. Develop other skills so your career doesn't end when your knees give out.

Type 7: The Character

You can't teach weird. Characters are born with it.

Unconventional. Impossible to categorize. They don't fit any traditional mold. They zig when everyone else zags. Their strangeness is their strength.

Characters stand out because they're memorable. In a sea of wrestlers who all look and act the same, they're the ones you can't forget. They might not be the best athletes or the best workers, but they have something nobody else has. Themselves.

They take creative risks that other wrestlers won't. They commit fully to gimmicks that seem crazy on paper. And somehow, through sheer force of originality, they make it work.

Being different cuts both ways.

Their uniqueness can limit their booking options. Some promoters don't know what to do with them. They can be too weird for mainstream success. They might struggle to be taken seriously as competitors. And if their gimmick stops working, they don't always have traditional skills to fall back on.

There's no template for Character gimmicks. Oddballs. Eccentrics. Cult favorites. The wrestler that fans either love or don't understand at all. Whatever makes you different is what you run with.

If you're a Character, your weirdness is your weapon. Don't try to fit in. Double down on what makes you different. Find the audience that gets you and build your career around them.

Orange Cassidy is one of the most over wrestlers in AEW, and he barely moves.

His whole gimmick is doing the absolute minimum. Lazy kicks. Hands in pockets. Sunglasses indoors. On paper, it shouldn't work. Every wrestling school in America teaches you to be intense, athletic, explosive.

But Orange Cassidy knew something about himself. He's naturally dry. Deadpan. His comedy timing is perfect because it's real. Instead of pretending to be a high energy babyface, he leaned all the way into who he actually is.

The result? He's one of the most popular wrestlers on the roster. He sells more merch than guys with twice his athleticism. He found his type and he owned it.

What's YOUR type? And are you leaning into it or fighting against it?

Type 8: The Talker

Give them two minutes and a microphone. That's all a Talker needs to own the building.

Articulate. Persuasive. Captivating on the microphone. They can talk people into buildings. They can make feuds feel personal. They can sell a match better than anyone.

Talkers are incredibly valuable because promos sell tickets. A great Talker can elevate an entire card. They can make average wrestlers seem like stars. They can be the mouthpiece that puts someone else over or the villain that everyone pays to see lose.

They understand words. They understand rhythm. They understand how to manipulate emotion through language. That's a rare skill.

Words only take you so far, though.

They might not be the best in the ring. They can rely too heavily on their verbal skills and neglect their wrestling. Fans might see them as all talk and no action. And in an era of short attention spans, they might not get the mic time they need to really shine.

Talkers dominate in roles like managers. Mouthpieces. Heels who run their mouth until someone shuts them up. Cult leaders. Manipulators. The voice of a faction.

Your words are your power. But don't neglect your ring work. The best Talkers can back it up when they need to. And consider management or commentary as career paths that let you maximize your gift.

Type 9: The Grinder

Talent burns bright and burns out. Grinders just keep going.

Consistent. Reliable. Professional. They might not be the most talented at any one thing, but they're solid at everything. They show up. They do the work. They never cause problems. They're the wrestlers who are still getting booked when the flashier guys have already burned out and disappeared.

Grinders build careers on dependability. Promoters know exactly what they're getting. No drama. No excuses. Just a professional who does their job every single time.

They understand that wrestling is a marathon, not a sprint. They pace themselves. They take care of their bodies. They make smart decisions. They're still standing when everyone else has fallen.

The trade-off?

They can be overlooked for more exciting wrestlers. They might never have the big moment or the viral clip. They can blend into the background. And they sometimes struggle with the self-promotion required to stand out because they're more comfortable just doing the work.

Grinders build careers as working class heroes. Veterans. Journeymen. The wrestler who earns everything the hard way.

Your consistency is your superpower. Don't compare yourself to flashier wrestlers. Play the long game. Be the person everyone can count on. Careers built on reliability last longer than careers built on hype.

Now that you've read through all nine types, it's time to figure out where you actually land.

I created a free worksheet to help you do this the right way. It walks you through the right questions, helps you identify your primary type, and shows you which secondary types you can build on. Don't just guess. Do the work.

Download it free at **prowrestlingskool.com**

Then come back and keep reading.

The Hybrid: Most Wrestlers Are a Combination

One more thing before you lock in your type.

Most wrestlers aren't just one type. They're a combination.

You might be a Powerhouse with Talker skills. A Daredevil with Fighter intensity. A Technician with a Character's weirdness. A Performer who thinks like a Thinker.

That's normal. That's actually an advantage.

The wrestlers who dominate usually have a primary type and one or two secondary types that make them more complete.

A Powerhouse who can also talk is more valuable than a Powerhouse who can't. A Daredevil who can also tell stories is more valuable than one who just does spots. A Grinder who has some Performer charisma will get more opportunities than one who blends into the background.

Your job is to identify your primary type first. That's your foundation. That's what you build on.

Then identify your secondary types. Those are your complementary skills. The things that make you more well-rounded.

Finally, identify the types that are NOT you. Those are the areas where you might need to improve, find partners who fill the gap, or simply avoid competing.

A Fighter trying to be a Technician will probably struggle. A Character trying to be a Powerhouse will look ridiculous. Know what you're not so you stop wasting energy forcing things that don't fit.

The magic formula is this: Lead with your primary type. Support it with your secondary types. Stop fighting against the types that aren't you.

That's how you build a career that feels natural and sustainable.

What Happens When You Fight Your Type

Chad Gable is one of the best technical wrestlers alive. He was an Olympic alternate. The guy can outwrestle almost anyone on the planet.

So what did WWE do with him? They gave him a gimmick called Shorty G. They put him in goofy shorts. They made his whole character about being short. Not about being a killer on the mat. Not about being a legitimate threat. Just... short.

It flopped. The crowd didn't care. Gable looked lost out there. You could see it in his face. He was playing a character that had nothing to do with who he actually was.

Then they finally let him be Alpha Academy's technical assassin. Suddenly he's cutting cocky promos about being better than everyone. Suddenly he's stretching people on the mat and talking trash while he does it. Suddenly the crowd is into it.

Same guy. Same skills. Different type. The only thing that changed was he stopped fighting who he really was.

Are you playing a character that fits who you really are? Or are you wearing someone else's gimmick?

Babyface Brain vs Heel Brain

Being a babyface or a heel isn't just about your character. It's about how your brain works.

Some wrestlers have a babyface brain. They naturally think in terms of fairness, respect, and doing things the right way. They want to earn success. They want people to like them. They play by the rules because the rules matter to them.

Some wrestlers have a heel brain. They naturally think in terms of results, leverage, and competitive advantage. They don't care about being liked. They care about winning. If bending the rules gets them ahead, they'll bend them without guilt.

Neither one is better than the other. But you need to know which one you have.

Because when you get it wrong, the cracks show fast.

A wrestler with a babyface brain tries to play a heel. They feel uncomfortable being booed. They soften their character without realizing it. They can't commit to being hated because deep down they want approval.

A wrestler with a heel brain tries to play a babyface. They come across as fake. Their promos feel forced. They can't connect with the crowd because they're performing emotions they don't actually feel.

The best wrestlers align their character with their brain.

Stone Cold Steve Austin had a heel brain in a babyface role. That's why he worked. He didn't play a traditional good guy. He played an antihero who did what he wanted. His heel brain made him feel authentic even when the crowd cheered him.

Know your brain. Build characters that match it.

Your Real Self vs Your Trained Self

Every wrestler has two selves.

Your real self is who you are naturally. Your personality. Your instincts. The things that come easy to you. The way you'd act if no one was watching.

Your trained self is who you were taught to be. The style your trainer emphasized. The moves you were told to do. The character choices you made because someone else suggested them.

Sometimes these two selves align. Your trainer saw your natural gifts and helped you develop them. Lucky you.

Sometimes they don't. Your trainer pushed you toward a style that doesn't fit. You learned to wrestle against your instincts. You developed habits that work against your natural strengths.

Signs you're working against your real self:

You feel exhausted after shows, not energized. Your promos feel scripted even when they're not. Crowds don't respond the way you expect. You watch your matches back and something feels off but you can't name it. You're doing everything right but nothing's clicking.

That's misalignment. You're wrestling as your trained self when you should be wrestling as your real self.

The fix isn't complicated. It just requires honesty.

Look at what comes naturally. Look at what feels forced. Build toward the natural. Unlearn the forced.

Early in my career, I tried to be an ex con character. Problem was, I'd never been to jail. I was playing a role that had nothing to do with who I actually was.

Meanwhile, I'm obsessed with horror films. I love blood and gore. I grew up watching slashers and thinking Jason Voorhees was the coolest thing on the planet. And offstage? I'm naturally goofy. I like making people laugh.

When I finally let those two things come together, the real Shank Dorsey was born. Hardcore wrestler. Horror fanatic. A little bit funny, a little bit dangerous. Suddenly people started to notice I existed. Not because I got better in the ring. Because I stopped pretending to be someone I wasn't.

That's what finding your type does. It makes you real. And real gets over.

When Your Character Matches Your Soul

The most successful wrestlers in history weren't acting.

They were playing amplified versions of themselves.

Stone Cold was Steve Austin turned up to eleven. The Rock was Dwayne Johnson with the charisma knob cranked to maximum.

CM Punk was Phil Brooks saying what he actually thought. John Cena is John Cena. The character and the man are the same.

When your character matches your soul, you can sustain it forever. You never have to remember your lines because you're just talking. You never have to remember your motivation because it's your real motivation. You're not performing. You're expressing.

When your character doesn't match your soul, you're always working. Every promo is an acting exercise. Every match is a performance. You're spending energy maintaining a mask instead of connecting with the crowd.

Some wrestlers can act their way through a career. Most can't.

The sustainable path is alignment. Find the character that lets you be yourself with the volume turned up. That's the character you can ride for decades.

The Foundation of Everything

Knowing your type is step one. But the reason it matters goes deeper than that.

Everything in this book builds on self-knowledge.

The laws of success only work when you apply them to your actual strengths. The advice about promoters only works when you know how you come across. The business strategies only work when you build a brand that's authentically you.

If you skip this step, everything else is harder.

If you nail this step, everything else flows.

You now know the nine types. You understand that most wrestlers are hybrids with a primary type and secondary types. You know your brain. You know the difference between your real self and your trained self. You know what alignment looks like.

That's the foundation.

Now we build.

CHAPTER 2
WHY KNOWING YOURSELF MATTERS

Most wrestlers think they know themselves.

They don't.

They know what they like. They know what moves they want to do. They know who they want to be like. But they don't know who they actually are.

And that gap is killing their career.

I've seen it a hundred times. A wrestler with real talent can't get booked. A wrestler with all the tools can't connect with crowds. A wrestler who works harder than anyone stays stuck in the same spot for years.

It's not bad luck. It's not politics. It's not the business holding them back.

It's that they don't know themselves.

They're blind to their own strengths. They don't see their own weaknesses. They have no idea what makes them special or what's holding them back.

Let's fix that.

What You Don't Know Is Hurting You

The things you don't know about yourself are the things that hurt you most.

If you knew you had a problem, you'd fix it. If you knew you were weak in some area, you'd work on it. If you knew what was holding you back, you'd stop doing it.

But you don't know. That's the problem.

You have blind spots. We all do. Parts of ourselves we can't see. Habits we don't notice. Patterns we repeat without thinking.

And in pro wrestling, those blind spots show up every time you step in the ring.

Maybe you cut off your opponent without realizing it. Maybe your promos run too long because you don't know when to stop. Maybe you have a look on your face that reads wrong on camera. Maybe you're stiff and don't know it. Maybe you're too soft and don't know it.

The crowd sees it. The promoter sees it. Your opponent sees it.

You don't.

That's why self-knowledge matters. You can't fix what you can't see. And you can't see it until you do the work of really looking at yourself.

The Mirror Lies

This gets tricky because of how your brain works.

When you look in the mirror, you don't see what everyone else sees.

You see the version of yourself you expect to see. The version you've built in your head over years. The version you want to be.

But that's not who you are on camera. That's not who you are in the ring. That's not who the crowd sees.

I've watched wrestlers cut promos in the mirror and think they look like Stone Cold. Then I watch the tape and they look like a guy trying too hard to be Stone Cold.

I've watched wrestlers throw punches that feel great to them. Then I watch the tape and the punches look fake.

I've watched wrestlers play characters they think are scary or cool or funny. Then I watch the tape and it's none of those things.

The mirror lies. The tape doesn't.

If you want to know yourself, you have to watch the tape. Not once. Over and over. With honest eyes. Looking for the things you don't want to see.

That's where the truth lives.

Finding Your Blind Spots

So how do you find what you can't see?

Three ways.

Watch the tape.

Record everything. Every match. Every promo. Every segment. Then watch it back. Not right after the show when you're still pumped up. Watch it the next day. Watch it with fresh eyes.

Look for patterns. What do you always do? What habits keep showing up? Where do you lose the crowd? Where do you get them back?

Don't just watch for the good stuff. Watch for the bad stuff. The moments that don't work. The spots that fell flat. The promos that went too long.

That's where your blind spots live.

Ask people who will tell you the truth.

Most people won't be honest with you. They'll tell you what you want to hear. They'll protect your feelings. They won't say the hard thing.

Find the people who will.

A good trainer. A trusted veteran. A friend who knows wrestling and isn't afraid to hurt your feelings. Someone who cares about your career more than they care about being liked.

Ask them: What am I doing wrong? What don't I see? What would you fix if you were me?

Then shut up and listen. Don't defend yourself. Don't explain. Just take it in.

Pay attention to what keeps happening.

Patterns don't lie.

If you keep not getting booked, there's a reason. If crowds keep going quiet during your matches, there's a reason. If opponents keep looking frustrated working with you, there's a reason.

Stop blaming bad luck. Start looking for the pattern.

What keeps happening? That's the clue. Follow it.

When Blind Spots Destroy Careers

Enzo Amore could talk.

Like, really talk. The guy was electric on the mic. "My name is Enzo Amore and I am a certified G and a bonafide stud, and you can't teach that." Crowds ate it up. He got himself more over than wrestlers with ten times his in-ring ability.

But Enzo had two blind spots that cost him everything.

First, he couldn't wrestle at a main event level and he didn't seem interested in fixing it. The locker room noticed. When you're getting pushed past guys who work harder and bump better, resentment builds fast.

Second, his attitude rubbed people the wrong way. Reports came out about heat with the locker room. Guys didn't want to work with him. He was eventually released from WWE, and no major promotion rushed to sign him.

One of the most over talkers in the company. Gone. Not because he lost his charisma. Because he couldn't see what was costing him respect behind the curtain.

What's the thing you can't see about yourself that's holding you back?

The Danger of Ego

Let's talk about something uncomfortable.

Ego.

Every wrestler has one. You need confidence to do this job. You need to believe in yourself. You need to think you're good.

But ego can also blind you.

Ego tells you that you're better than you are. Ego tells you that the problem is always someone else. Ego tells you that you don't need feedback because you already know what you're doing.

Ego is a liar.

I've seen talented wrestlers destroy their careers because their ego wouldn't let them hear the truth. They thought they knew better than everyone. They wouldn't listen to trainers. They wouldn't take advice. They blamed promoters, blamed politics, blamed everyone but themselves.

And they stayed stuck. Or they flamed out.

The wrestlers who make it are the ones who can set their ego aside. They can hear hard truths. They can admit when they're wrong. They can look at themselves honestly even when it hurts.

This doesn't mean you have no confidence. It means your confidence is real, not fake. Real confidence can handle criticism. Fake confidence crumbles when challenged.

Check your ego at the door. It's the only way to really know yourself.

When You Finally See It

Cody Rhodes was Stardust.

If you don't remember, that's the point. WWE had him painted up in face paint, playing a cosmic weirdo, doing comedy bits. He was Dusty Rhodes' son. He had the bloodline, the talent, the look. And he was stuck in a gimmick with a ceiling.

What made Cody different? He finally saw it.

He knew Stardust wasn't going to get him where he wanted to go. He asked for his release. WWE granted it. And suddenly the son of the American Dream was working indie shows, betting his entire career on a truth he'd finally admitted to himself.

What had been holding him back? He'd been playing it safe. Waiting for WWE to hand him an opportunity instead of creating his own. Accepting gimmicks that didn't fit because that's what good employees do.

Once he saw it, he fixed it. He went to the indies and became a top guy. He helped build AEW from scratch. He became a bigger star outside WWE than he ever was inside. Then he went back on his own terms and main evented WrestleMania. Twice.

Same talent he always had. The only thing that changed was he stopped lying to himself about what was holding him back.

What are you accepting right now that you know isn't getting you where you want to go?

Your Strengths

Once you start seeing yourself clearly, you need to figure out two things.

Your strengths and your weaknesses.

Let's start with strengths.

Your strengths are the things that come easy to you. The things you do better than most people without even trying. The things that feel natural.

Some wrestlers are naturally funny. Some are naturally scary. Some move like athletes. Some tell stories without saying a word. Some connect with crowds the moment they walk through the curtain.

These are strengths.

The problem is most wrestlers don't lean into their strengths. They take them for granted. They spend all their time trying to fix weaknesses instead of making their strengths even stronger.

That's backwards.

Your strengths are your money. Your strengths are what make you different. Your strengths are why someone would book you over the hundred other wrestlers who want that spot.

If you're funny, be funnier. If you're intense, be more intense. If you're athletic, show off your body. If you're a great talker, talk more.

Don't hide your strengths. Blast them. Make them so obvious that nobody can miss them.

How to Find Your Strengths

Some wrestlers don't know what their strengths are. They've never thought about it. Or they're so focused on what they can't do that they miss what they can do.

Try these four tests.

What do people praise you for?

Pay attention to what people say after your matches. Not the generic "good job" stuff. The specific stuff. "Man, your facials are great." "That promo was fire." "The way you sell is so believable."

When multiple people praise the same thing, that's a strength.

What feels easy to you?

Strengths usually feel easy. They don't take a lot of effort. You do them without thinking. Other people struggle with things that come natural to you.

What parts of wrestling feel easy? That's probably where your strengths live.

What do you do that others don't?

Look at wrestlers at your level. What do you do that they can't do as well? What sets you apart? What's different about you?

That difference is often a strength waiting to be developed.

What did you do before wrestling?

A lot of strengths come from outside wrestling. Maybe you played football and you're naturally physical. Maybe you did theater and you understand performance. Maybe you were a class clown and you have natural comedic timing.

Your life before wrestling gave you skills. Those skills can become strengths in the ring.

Your Weaknesses

Now let's talk about weaknesses.

Your weaknesses are the things you struggle with. The things that don't come easy. The things you have to force.

Every wrestler has them. Even the greats.

Some wrestlers can't talk. Some can't work long matches. Some have no charisma. Some are sloppy in the ring. Some can't connect with crowds.

These are weaknesses.

And most wrestlers handle them wrong.

They try to fix all of them. They spend hours working on things they're bad at. They grind away at skills that don't come natural.

And they stay average at everything.

That's a trap.

The truth is you don't need to fix every weakness. You just need to manage them.

If you can't talk, get a manager. If you can't work long matches, work short ones. If you have no charisma, lean into being intense and serious. If you're sloppy, drill the basics until you're at least safe.

You don't need to be great at everything. You need to be great at a few things and not terrible at the rest.

Know your weaknesses. Manage them. But don't let them eat all your time and energy. Your strengths are where the money is.

The Weakness That Will Kill Your Career

Not all weaknesses are equal.

Some weaknesses are minor. They hold you back a little but they won't destroy you. You can work around them.

Some weaknesses are major. They will end your career if you don't address them.

These are the ones you cannot ignore:

Being unsafe. If you hurt people, your career is over. Promoters won't book you. Wrestlers won't work with you. Word spreads fast. Being unsafe is a career killer.

Being unreliable. If you no-show, show up late, or can't be counted on, you won't get booked. Promoters need people they can trust. If you're unreliable, you're done.

Being difficult. If you're a pain to work with, word gets around. Drama follows you. Promoters don't want headaches. They'll book someone else.

Having no presence. If crowds don't react to you at all, that's a problem. You can be a heel they hate or a babyface they love. But if they feel nothing, you've got work to do.

These weaknesses must be fixed. They're not optional. They're the basics of being a professional.

Everything else can be managed. These cannot.

Your Money Spot

Every successful wrestler has one thing they do better than almost anyone else. The thing that makes people react. The thing that makes promoters want to book them. The thing that makes fans remember them.

That's your money spot.

It might be a move. It might be a look. It might be how you talk. It might be how you make people feel.

The greats all had one.

Stone Cold had the Stunner and the middle fingers. Ric Flair had the strut and the "Wooo." Undertaker had the entrance and the sit-up. Hulk Hogan had the comeback and the leg drop.

These were money spots. The things crowds came to see. The things that made them stars.

What's your money spot?

If you don't know, that's a problem. If you don't have one, that's an even bigger problem.

Finding your money spot is one of the most important things you can do for your career. It's the thing you build everything else around.

And it usually lives in your strengths. The thing you do better than anyone else. The thing that feels most natural. The thing that gets the best reactions.

Find it. Own it. Make it yours.

Developing Your Money Spot

Once you find your money spot, you have to develop it.

This means doing it over and over until it's perfect. Until it's yours. Until nobody does it better than you.

Your money spot should be so good that people talk about it. So good that fans wait for it. So good that it becomes part of your identity.

This takes time. This takes reps. This takes paying attention to what works and what doesn't.

Watch the crowd when you hit your money spot. Do they react? Do they pop? Do they care?

If yes, keep refining it. Make it sharper. Make it bigger. Make it more you.

If no, something's wrong. Maybe it's the timing. Maybe it's the setup. Maybe it's not actually your money spot and you need to find something else.

Your money spot is your signature. It's what people remember about you. It's what makes you money.

Develop it until it's undeniable.

The Blind Spot That Almost Ended Me

During my Shank Dorsey era, I was a mess.

Out of shape. Overweight. Unhealthy. I drank. I smoked. Pretty much everything a professional athlete shouldn't do. I couldn't see it at the time because I was having fun and getting booked. But my body was keeping score.

At age 30, I walked away from pro wrestling. My body couldn't take it anymore.

Thirteen years later, I started New Ohio Wrestling as a promoter. I was 43, running shows from behind the scenes, watching other people do what I used to do. And something hit me. I'd spent years blaming my body for giving out when the truth was I'd never taken care of it in the first place.

That was my blind spot. I treated wrestling like a hobby and my body like a trash can. Then I wondered why my career ended early.

So I fixed it. I started the WrestleFit Training & Lifestyle Center. I got myself a coach. I went from 308 pounds down to 225. I quit smoking. I stopped drinking. I became the athlete I should have been twenty years earlier.

At 53 years old, I had my first full blown singles match in decades. And it went great. I was sore the next day, but I finished. A few years before that, I couldn't have lasted two minutes without seriously hurting myself.

I haven't smoked in 20 years. I rarely touch alcohol anymore.

Same person. Same love for wrestling. The only thing that changed was I finally saw what I'd been doing to myself and decided to fix it.

What's the thing you're doing to yourself right now that you're pretending isn't a problem?

Self-Knowledge Is a Competitive Advantage

Self-knowledge is rare.

Most people go through life without ever really knowing themselves. They react. They drift. They do what feels good in the moment without understanding why.

Wrestlers are the same. Most of them never do this work. They never look hard at themselves. They never figure out their type, their strengths, their weaknesses, their money spot.

Which means if you do this work, you have an advantage.

You'll make better decisions because you understand yourself. You'll build a better character because it fits who you really are. You'll focus on the right things because you know where your money is.

While other wrestlers are spinning their wheels trying to be something they're not, you'll be building on a solid foundation.

The Work Most Wrestlers Won't Do

Most wrestlers won't do this work.

They won't watch their videos honestly. They won't ask for real feedback. They won't look at their blind spots. They won't admit their weaknesses. They won't check their ego.

It's too hard. It's too painful. It's easier to blame the business.

That's why most wrestlers stay stuck.

But you're reading this book. You're different. You're willing to do the hard thing.

So do it.

Watch your videos. Ask for feedback. Find your blind spots. Know your strengths. Know your weaknesses. Find your money spot. Develop it until it's undeniable.

Do the work that most wrestlers won't do.

That's how you get the results that most wrestlers won't get.

The Foundation Is Set

Part One is complete. You know your type. You know your brain. You know how to find what you can't see. You know where your money spot lives.

That's the groundwork.

Now it's time to learn the laws that will make you successful.

The laws start now.

PART TWO
PRO WRESTLING LAWS OF SUCCESS

CHAPTER 3
LAW #1 – PICK YOUR MISSION

Ask a pro wrestler what they want and watch them freeze.

They say they want to "make it." They say they want to be a "star." They say they want to "succeed in wrestling."

But what does that mean?

Ask them to be specific and they freeze. Ask them what success looks like for them and they give vague answers. Ask them where they want to be in five years and they shrug.

That's the problem.

You can't hit a target you can't see. You can't reach a goal you haven't set. You can't build a career if you don't know what you're building toward.

You need a mission. And this law shows you how to find one.

The Power of Knowing What You Want

When you know exactly what you want, every decision gets easier.

Should I take this booking? Does it move me toward my goal or away from it? Should I do this gimmick? Does it fit my mission? Should I work with this promoter? Will it help me get where I'm going?

When you have a clear mission, you have a filter. Things either fit or they don't. Yes or no. Simple.

When you don't have a clear mission, everything is confusing. Every choice feels hard. You second-guess yourself. You take opportunities that waste your time. You say yes to things that pull you off course.

Clarity is power.

The wrestlers who make it almost always know what they want. They can tell you exactly where they're going. They have a picture in their head. A target they're aiming at.

The wrestlers who stay stuck almost never know what they want. They're just "trying to make it." They're hoping something good happens. They're waiting for someone else to give them direction.

Hope is not a strategy. Waiting is not a plan.

You need a mission.

What Is a Mission?

Your mission is your purpose. Your direction. The thing you're working toward.

It's not a dream. Dreams are fuzzy. Dreams are wishes. Dreams are things you think about before you fall asleep.

A mission is concrete. A mission is clear. A mission is something you can actually work toward.

Compare these:

Dream: "I want to be famous."

Mission: "I want to be the top heel in the Midwest indie scene within three years."

Dream: "I want to make money wrestling."

Mission: "I want to make $5,000 a month from wrestling and wrestling-related income within two years."

Dream: "I want to be like my favorite wrestler."

Mission: "I want to build a character that gets me booked on 50 shows a year and builds a fanbase of 10,000 followers."

See the difference?

Dreams are vague. Missions are specific.

Dreams have no deadline. Missions have a timeline.

Dreams are about wishing. Missions are about working.

You need to turn your dreams into missions. That's how they become real.

The One-Sentence Mission

Try this exercise. It might be the most important thing you do with this book.

Write your mission in one sentence.

Not a paragraph. Not a page. One sentence.

This forces you to get clear. You can't hide behind vague words when you only have one sentence. You have to know exactly what you want.

A good mission sentence has three parts.

1. *What you want to achieve.* This is the goal. The outcome. The thing you're working toward.
2. *Who you want to be.* This is your identity. Your character. How you want to be known.
3. *When you want to achieve it.* This is your timeline. Your deadline. The date you're aiming for.

Put them together and you get something like this:

"I want to be the most booked comedy wrestler in Ohio within two years."

"I want to build a heel character that gets me signed to a TV deal within three years."

"I want to make $3,000 a month from wrestling and online income within 18 months."

"I want to be known as the best technical wrestler on the indie scene within two years."

"I want to run my own promotion that draws 500 fans per show within five years."

Each of these is clear. Each of these is specific. Each of these gives you something to work toward.

What's your one sentence?

Don't skip this part.

Most wrestlers read through this chapter and think they've got it figured out. They don't write anything down. They keep the mission floating around in their head where it's fuzzy and easy to ignore.

That's not a mission. That's a wish.

I created a free Mission Builder Worksheet that walks you through this the right way. It forces you to get specific. By the time you're done, you'll have your mission written in one clear sentence that you can put on your wall, your phone, or your mirror.

Download it free at **prowrestlingskool.com**

Then come back and finish the chapter.

Different Missions for Different Wrestlers

Not every wrestler wants the same thing. And that's okay.

Some wrestlers want to be world champion. They want the big stage. They want the bright lights. They want to main event in front of thousands.

Some wrestlers want to be the best worker. They don't care about fame. They care about the craft. They want to have great matches and earn respect from their peers.

Some wrestlers want freedom. They want to make enough money to quit their day job. They want to control their schedule. They want wrestling to give them a life they love.

Some wrestlers want to build a business. They want to own a promotion. They want to train the next generation. They want to create something that lasts.

Some wrestlers want to entertain. They want to make people laugh. They want to give fans a good time. They want to be remembered for bringing joy.

All of these are valid missions. None of them is better than the others.

The mistake is chasing someone else's mission. Wanting something because you think you're supposed to want it. Trying to be a world champion when what you really want is freedom.

Your mission has to be yours. Not your trainer's. Not your favorite wrestler's. Not what you think sounds impressive.

What do you actually want? Be honest. That's your mission.

Your Character Is Your Career Plan

Most wrestlers treat their character like it's separate from their career. It's not.

Your character is your career plan.

Your character decides what promoters think of you. It decides what fans think of you. It decides what kind of bookings you get. It decides what kind of money you make. It decides what kind of career you have.

If you play a comedy character, you'll get booked for comedy spots. If you play a monster heel, you'll get booked to make babyfaces look good. If you play a technical wizard, you'll get booked for clinics. If you play a main event star, you'll get booked like one.

Your character shapes everything.

So when you pick your character, you're really picking your career path. You're deciding what kind of wrestler you want to be. What kind of bookings you want to get. What kind of money you want to make.

Most wrestlers pick characters without thinking about this. They pick what sounds cool. They pick what their favorite wrestler does. They pick whatever comes to mind.

Then they wonder why their career isn't going where they want.

Your character should match your mission. If your mission is to be a main event star, your character should be a main event character. If your mission is to be the best comedy act on the indies, your character should be built for comedy. If your mission is to get signed to a TV deal, your character should be TV-ready.

Character and mission have to match. If they don't, you're working against yourself.

The Problem With No Mission

Let me tell you what happens when you don't have a mission.

You drift.

You take whatever bookings come your way. You work for whoever calls. You do whatever gimmick sounds fun this week. You have no direction. No purpose. No plan.

And you end up going in circles.

I've seen wrestlers work for ten years and end up right where they started. Same level. Same bookings. Same money. Nothing changed.

Not because they didn't work hard. They worked their tails off. But they worked without direction. They put in effort without purpose. They ran fast but went nowhere.

That's what happens without a mission.

You can work hard and still fail. You can put in years and have nothing to show for it. You can love wrestling with all your heart and still end up broke and bitter.

Hard work alone isn't enough. You need hard work aimed at something. You need effort with direction. You need a mission.

When Talent Meets No Direction

Lex Luger had everything.

The look. The body. The athleticism. He was handmade to be a world champion. WWE wanted him. WCW wanted him. He got pushed harder than almost anyone in his era.

But Luger never seemed to know what he wanted.

He bounced from WCW to WWE and back again. He went from heel to face to heel without ever fully committing. One year he's the "Narcissist" obsessed with his own body. The next year he's the "All American" slamming Yokozuna on a battleship. Then he's back in WCW running with the nWo. Then against them. Then who knows.

Every time it looked like he was about to become THE guy, something stalled out. Not because of injuries. Not because of politics. Because he never locked in on a mission and rode it all the way.

Compare that to guys with half his physical gifts who became legends because they knew exactly who they were and where they were going. Luger had every tool. But tools without direction just sit in a box.

Talent doesn't guarantee success. A clear mission does.

Do you know exactly what you're building toward? Or are you just going wherever the wind blows?

The Problem With the Wrong Mission

Having a mission is important. But having the right mission matters even more.

Some wrestlers pick missions that are wrong for them.

They pick missions based on what other people want. Their trainer's vision. Their parents' expectations. What they think they're supposed to want.

They pick missions based on ego. Being a world champion. Being famous. Being the best. Not because they really want it, but because it sounds good.

They pick missions that don't fit who they are. A Grinder trying to be a main event star. A Character trying to be taken seriously as a technician. A Talker trying to be a high-flyer.

Wrong missions lead to frustration. You're chasing something that doesn't fit. You're working toward a goal that won't make you happy even if you reach it.

The right mission matches who you are. It fits your type. It plays to your strengths. It excites you when you think about it. It feels right in your gut.

Don't pick a mission because it sounds impressive. Pick a mission because it's yours.

How to Know If Your Mission Is Right

When you think about your mission, how do you feel?

If you feel excited, energized, and motivated, it's probably right.

If you feel stressed, pressured, or like you're trying to prove something, it might be wrong.

The right mission pulls you forward. It makes you want to do the work. It gets you out of bed. It keeps you going when things get hard.

The wrong mission feels like a weight. It drains you. It makes the work feel like a chore. It makes you want to quit.

Pay attention to how you feel. Your gut knows things your brain doesn't.

Another test: *Is this mission for you or for someone else?*

Some wrestlers chase missions because they want to prove something to their parents. Or their old trainer. Or the kids who made fun of them. Or the promoter who said they'd never make it.

That's not a mission. That's revenge. And revenge is a terrible fuel for a career.

Your mission should be for you. Because you want it. Because it matters to you. Because it's the life you want to live.

Not because you're trying to prove something to someone who probably isn't even watching.

The Power of Writing It Down

This sounds too simple to matter, but it does.

Writing down your mission makes it more real.

There's something about putting words on paper that changes things in your brain. A mission that lives only in your head is easy to forget. Easy to change. Easy to ignore.

A mission that's written down stares back at you. It holds you accountable. It reminds you what you said you wanted.

Write your mission down. Put it somewhere you'll see it every day. On your mirror. On your phone. On your wall.

Read it every morning. Let it sink in. Let it shape your day.

The wrestlers who write down their missions are more likely to achieve them than the wrestlers who don't.

Write it down.

Mission and the 3R Framework

Remember the 3R Framework from the introduction?

Reach. Reputation. Revenue.

Your mission should connect to all three.

Reach: How will your mission help you grow your audience? How will it get you in front of more people? How will it make you more visible?

Reputation: How will your mission build your reputation? What will people say about you? How will you be known?

Revenue: How will your mission make you money? What income will it create? How will it lead to financial freedom?

A good mission hits all three. It grows your audience. It builds your reputation. It makes you money.

A weak mission might hit one or two but miss the others. You might get famous but stay broke. You might make money but have no fans. You might have a great reputation but nobody knows who you are.

Check your mission against the 3Rs. Make sure it covers all the bases.

Breaking Your Mission Into Pieces

A mission without a plan is just a wish.

Once you have your mission, you need to break it into smaller pieces. Things you can actually do. Steps you can actually take.

Say your mission is to be the top heel in your region in three years. What has to happen? You need to get booked on more shows. You need to develop your character. You need to build a fanbase. You need to get noticed by the right promoters.

Each of those is a smaller goal. And each of those can be broken down even more.

How do you get booked on more shows? Reach out to promoters. Have a good media kit to show them. Be easy to work with so they book you again.

How do you develop your character? Watch your matches and find what works. Practice your promos. Get feedback from people you trust.

See how this works?

The big mission breaks into smaller goals. The smaller goals break into action steps. The action steps are things you can do this week. Today. Right now.

That's how missions become real. Not by wishing. By breaking them down and doing the work.

Missions Are Not Set in Stone

Your mission can change.

What you want at 20 might not be what you want at 30. What excites you today might bore you in five years. Where you're trying to go now might not be where you want to end up.

That's okay.

Your mission isn't a life sentence. It's a direction. And directions can change as you grow and learn.

The point isn't to pick the perfect mission right now and never change it. The point is to have a mission so you have direction. So you're not drifting. So you're working toward something.

Check in with your mission every year. Does it still fit? Does it still excite you? Is it still where you want to go?

If yes, keep going. If no, adjust.

A changing mission isn't failure. It's growth. It means you learned something about yourself. It means you're paying attention.

Just don't change your mission every week. That's not growth. That's drifting with extra steps.

Pick a mission. Work toward it. Check in once a year. Adjust if needed. Keep going.

When Mission Meets Execution

The Rock didn't just want to be a wrestler.

He wanted to be the most electrifying man in sports entertainment. Then he wanted to be the biggest movie star on the planet. He said it out loud. He worked toward it every single day. Everything he did served that mission.

His promos weren't just entertaining. They were building a brand that could translate to Hollywood. His matches weren't just good. They were showcases for a personality bigger than wrestling. His choices weren't random. They were calculated steps toward becoming Dwayne Johnson, global entertainment empire.

Look at where he is now. One of the highest paid actors in the world. A business empire. Co-owner of the UFL football league. Board member at TKO, the company that owns both WWE and UFC. The guy turned a wrestling career into a billion dollar brand.

That doesn't happen by accident. That happens when you know exactly what you want and you build everything toward it.

The Rock had a mission. And he never stopped working it.

What's your mission? And is everything you're doing right now moving you toward it?

The Courage to Choose

Nobody talks about this part, but picking a mission takes courage.

When you pick a mission, you're committing. You're saying "this is what I want" out loud. You're putting yourself on the line.

That's scary.

What if you fail? What if you pick the wrong thing? What if people judge you for what you want?

These fears keep most wrestlers from ever picking a mission. They stay vague on purpose. They don't commit because commitment feels risky.

But staying vague is the biggest risk of all. It guarantees you'll drift. It guarantees you'll waste time. It guarantees you'll look back with regret.

Picking a mission might mean you fail at something specific. But not picking a mission means you fail at everything by default.

Have the courage to choose. Have the courage to commit. Have the courage to say "this is what I want" and go after it.

That's how careers are built.

My Mission

When I was wrestling as Shank Dorsey, I didn't have a mission.

I was just going. Show to show. Booking to booking. Trying to make something happen without knowing what that something was. I was busy, but I wasn't building anything. I was moving, but I wasn't going anywhere specific.

I didn't realize it at the time. I thought working hard was enough. I thought if I just kept showing up, something would click. But hard work without direction is just spinning your wheels.

When I came back to pro wrestling as a promoter and trainer, everything changed. I finally got clear on what I was building toward.

My mission is to make pro wrestling better than I found it.

I want to show people in this business how to treat it like a business. Not a fantasy. Not a way to look cool in front of your friends. A real business that can support a real life.

I want to change the mindset of wrestlers who think the only path to going fulltime is signing a big contract with a major promotion. There's another way. You can build it yourself. You can own your income. You can create freedom without waiting for someone to hand it to you.

That's my mission. Everything I do now serves it. This book. Pro Wrestling Skool. The training. The promotion. All of it points in the same direction.

Once I got clear on that, everything got easier. I stopped saying yes to things that didn't fit. I started building instead of just working.

What's your mission? Can you say it in one sentence?

Pick Your Mission

This is the first pro wrestling law of success for a reason.

Everything else builds on this. All the other laws only work if you have a direction. All the strategies only help if you know where you're going.

Pick your mission.

Get clear on what you want. Write it in one sentence. Make sure it fits who you are. Make sure it connects to Reach, Reputation, and Revenue. Break it into smaller pieces. Write it down where you'll see it every day.

Then commit to it.

Not halfway. Not "I'll try." Full commitment. This is what I'm working toward. This is where I'm going. This is who I'm becoming.

That's Law #1. Pick your mission.

Without it, nothing else matters.

CHAPTER 4
LAW #2 – BELIEVE IN YOURSELF

The crowd knows.

They always know.

You can have the best gear. The coolest entrance. The sickest moves. But if you don't believe in yourself, the crowd will feel it. They won't know why they don't care about you. They just won't care.

I've seen it a hundred times. A wrestler walks through the curtain looking like a star. Great music. Great look. Everything perfect on the surface.

But something's off.

The crowd sits on their hands. The reactions don't come. The match falls flat. Everyone feels it but nobody can name it.

I can name it.

The wrestler didn't believe.

Deep down, underneath the gear and the music and the character, they didn't believe they belonged. They didn't believe they were good enough. They didn't believe they deserved to be there.

And the crowd picked up on it. They always do.

Nobody teaches this in wrestling school. But it might be the most important thing you ever learn.

You Can't Fake It

You can't fake belief.

You can fake moves. You can fake pain. You can fake anger and sadness and joy. Wrestling is built on faking things.

But you can't fake believing in yourself.

It comes through in everything you do. How you walk. How you stand. How you look at your opponent. How you hold yourself when you're not doing anything.

A wrestler who believes moves different than a wrestler who doesn't. They take up more space. They move with purpose. They don't rush. They don't apologize with their body language.

A wrestler who doesn't believe shrinks. They move too fast. They look away. They fill silence with nervous energy. They apologize before they've done anything wrong.

The crowd reads this in seconds. Before you throw your first punch. Before you say your first word. They've already decided if you're somebody or nobody.

And they decide based on whether you think you're somebody or nobody.

You can't fake it. You have to actually mean it.

What Belief Looks Like

Picture this.

Two wrestlers stand in the ring for a staredown. Same size. Same build. Same experience level.

Wrestler A looks at his opponent. Really looks. Eyes locked. Not blinking. Not fidgeting. Just standing there like he owns the ring. Like this is his house and his opponent is just visiting.

Wrestler B looks at his opponent too. But his eyes dart around. He shifts his weight. He adjusts his gear. He glances at the crowd. He looks like he's waiting for permission to be there.

Who does the crowd think is going to win?

Wrestler A. Every time.

Not because he's bigger. Not because he's better. Because he carries himself like he belongs there and Wrestler B doesn't.

That's what it looks like. It's not arrogance. It's not cockiness. It's quiet certainty. It's knowing you belong. It's standing in the ring like you've already won and you're just waiting for everyone else to catch up.

You can't teach that with drills. You can't learn it from watching tape. You have to build it from the inside out.

Where Belief Comes From

Most people think confidence comes from success. You win some matches, you get some pops, and then you start believing in yourself.

That's backwards.

Belief comes first. Success comes second.

You have to believe before you have proof. You have to feel like a star before anyone treats you like one. You have to know you belong before anyone tells you that you do.

This is hard. It feels fake at first. It feels like you're lying to yourself.

But it's not fake. It's how the mind works.

Your brain doesn't know the difference between real confidence and practiced confidence. If you act like you belong, your brain starts to accept it. If you carry yourself like a star, your brain starts to think you're a star.

And then your actions change. And then your results change. And then the confidence becomes real.

It starts as a choice. You choose to believe before you have evidence. You choose to act like you belong before anyone says you do.

That's where it comes from. Not from success. From decision.

The Voice in Your Head

Every wrestler has a voice in their head.

Sometimes that voice helps. It tells you that you're good. That you can do this. That you belong.

Sometimes that voice hurts. It tells you that you're not good enough. That everyone is better than you. That you're going to fail.

The voice that wins is the voice you feed.

The voice that gets your attention is the voice that runs your life.

If you spend your time focused on doubt and failure, that voice wins. If you focus on your strengths and your wins, that voice wins instead.

We'll go deeper on how to train that voice in Chapter 12. For now, understand this: the voice you feed is the voice that grows.

Most wrestlers feed the wrong voice without even realizing it.

And they wonder why they don't believe in themselves.

You have to feed the right voice. On purpose. Every day.

When Talent Meets Doubt

Jake Roberts might be the most talented wrestler who never became world champion.

"The Snake" could cut a promo that made your skin crawl. His psychology in the ring was years ahead of everyone else. He understood storytelling better than wrestlers twice as decorated. The DDT was one of the most protected finishers in wrestling history.

But Jake never believed he deserved the top spot.

You could see it in interviews. You could hear it when he talked about his career. Behind the brilliance was a man fighting demons, and the biggest demon was the voice in his head telling him he wasn't good enough. He's been open about his struggles with addiction, his childhood trauma, his battles with self-worth.

The talent was undeniable. The belief wasn't there.

Jake influenced generations of wrestlers. His promos are studied like film school lectures. But he never held the world title. He never got the crowning moment his talent deserved.

Not because the business held him back. Because something inside him did.

Talent without belief is a tragedy. Jake Roberts is proof.

What voice are you listening to?

The Crowd Reads Everything

This will either scare you or free you.

The crowd reads everything.

Not just your moves. Not just your words. Everything.

They read your posture. They read your eyes. They read how you breathe. They read the tiny moments between the moves. They read what you do when you're not doing anything.

Most of this happens below the surface. The crowd isn't thinking about it. They're just feeling it. They feel something about you and they react to that feeling.

When you believe in yourself, the crowd feels it. They lean in. They care. They invest in what you're doing.

When you don't, they feel that too. They check out. They get bored. They stop caring.

This is why two wrestlers can do the exact same match and get completely different reactions. One believes. One doesn't. The crowd feels the difference.

You can't hide from this. You can't trick the crowd. They read everything.

The only answer is to actually believe.

Belief Is Not Arrogance

Belief is not arrogance.

Arrogance is thinking you're better than everyone else. Arrogance is refusing to learn. Arrogance is acting like you have nothing to improve.

Belief is different.

Belief is knowing you belong. Trusting your skills. Feeling worthy of the spot you're in.

You can believe in yourself and still be humble. You can believe in yourself and still learn from others. You can believe in yourself and still see your weaknesses.

In fact, real belief makes you more humble. When you truly believe in yourself, you don't need to prove it to anyone. You don't need to put others down. You don't need to act like you know everything.

Arrogance is fake belief. It's what people do when they're trying to convince themselves they're good enough. It's loud because it's empty.

Real belief is quiet. It doesn't need to announce itself. It just is.

Be confident, not cocky. Believe, but stay hungry. Know your worth, but keep learning.

That's the balance.

The Power of Reps

One of the best ways to build belief is through reps.

Every time you do something well, your confidence grows a little. Every time you hit a move clean. Every time you get a reaction from the crowd. Every time you cut a good promo.

Reps build belief.

This is why training matters so much. Not just for your skills. For your mind. Every rep you take is a deposit in your confidence account. You're proving to yourself that you can do this.

The wrestlers who train the most usually believe the most. Not because they're arrogant. Because they've put in so many reps that their body knows it can do the job.

If you're struggling with doubt, train more. Take more reps. Do the work until your body believes even when your mind has questions.

Your body will drag your mind along. Put in the reps and the rest will follow.

Count the Small Wins

Most wrestlers only count the big moments. The title match. The main event. The huge pop.

But small wins matter more.

Did you hit all your spots clean? Small win. Did a fan ask for a picture? Small win. Did a promoter say you did good work? Small win. Did you get through a promo without freezing? Small win.

These add up.

Every small win is evidence that you belong. Every small win is proof that you can do this. Every small win feeds the voice that says you're good enough.

Start counting your small wins. Write them down if you have to. Train your brain to notice them.

Most wrestlers ignore small wins and obsess over failures. They have a hundred good moments and one bad one, and they only remember the bad one.

Flip that. Notice the wins. Let them stack up.

Preparation Is Confidence

Nothing kills belief faster than being unprepared.

If you don't know your spots, you won't trust yourself during the match. If you haven't practiced your promo, you won't trust yourself on the mic. If you're out of shape, you won't trust yourself when you're gassed.

Preparation builds belief.

When you've done the work, you know you can trust yourself. When you've drilled the spots a hundred times, you know they'll be there when you need them. When you've practiced your promo until it's second nature, you know you won't freeze.

That's real confidence. Not hoping you'll be good. Knowing you will because you prepared.

The wrestlers who believe the most are usually the wrestlers who prepare the most. They leave nothing to chance. They do the work so they can trust themselves when the lights come on.

If you want to believe in yourself, prepare like your career depends on it. Because it does.

The Mental Game

Wrestling is a mental game more than most people realize.

Everyone sees the physical part. The bumps. The moves. The athleticism.

But the mental part is what separates good from great.

The great wrestlers have mastered their minds. They can control their thoughts. They can manage their emotions. They can perform under pressure because they've trained their brain just like they trained their body.

The average wrestlers haven't done this work. They're at the mercy of their thoughts. When doubt creeps in, they fall apart. When nerves hit, they shrink. When things go wrong, they spiral.

Belief is what separates the wrestlers who make it from the ones who don't. There's no in between.

The good news is belief can be built. It's a skill, not a gift.

But you have to practice it on purpose. And it starts with what happens next.

Making It Look Real

Wrestling is about making things look real. The punches aren't real (*most of the time*). The pain isn't real (*agree to disagree*). The hatred isn't real (*sometimes*). But it has to look real or nobody cares.

Belief is what makes it look real.

When you believe in your character, the character looks real. When you believe in the story, the story looks real. When you believe you're in a fight, the fight looks real.

The crowd can tell when a wrestler is just going through the motions. They can tell when someone doesn't buy what they're selling. It looks fake. It feels fake.

But when a wrestler truly commits? Magic happens. The crowd forgets it's a show. They get lost in the story. They react like it's real.

That's the power of commitment. It makes fake things feel true.

The best wrestlers aren't the best actors. They're the best believers. They commit so deeply to what they're doing that the crowd commits too.

If you want your work to look real, you have to buy in completely. Not surface level. Deep down.

That's how you connect. That's how you get over.

When Things Go Wrong

The real test isn't whether you believe when everything is going right. That's easy.

The test is whether you can hold it together when things fall apart.

What about when you botch a move? What about when the crowd is dead? What about when you're hurt or tired or things aren't going your way?

Can you still carry yourself like you belong?

The great wrestlers can. They mess up and keep going like nothing happened. They work dead crowds like they're main eventing WrestleMania. They fight through pain and fatigue without losing their edge.

Their confidence doesn't depend on outside circumstances. It comes from inside. It's unshakeable.

That's what you're building toward. Belief that doesn't need everything to be perfect. Belief that holds up when things fall apart. Belief that carries you through the hard times.

That kind of inner strength takes years to build. You build it one rep at a time. One small win at a time. One hard night at a time.

But once you have it, nobody can take it from you.

When Belief Changes Everything

Becky Lynch believed she was a main eventer when nobody else did.

For years, WWE treated her like a supporting character. She was Charlotte's friend. She was the one who came up short. She was talented, sure, but not the one they were building around.

Becky didn't accept that story.

She started calling herself "The Man." She started carrying herself like the top star in the company. She cut promos like she was the most important person on the roster. She believed it so hard that the crowd started believing it too.

WWE didn't hand her the main event of WrestleMania. She took it. She willed herself into a spot that wasn't supposed to be hers.

Look at what that takes. Everyone around you is saying you're a mid-carder. The booking says you're a mid-carder. The storylines say you're a mid-carder. And you just... decide you're not. You decide you're the main event. And you act like it until reality catches up.

That's belief. Not hoping. Not wishing. Deciding.

Becky Lynch became "The Man" because she believed she was "The Man" before anyone gave her permission.

What would happen if you believed in yourself that hard?

The Moment I Almost Lost It

I always believed I was good enough to be a wrestler.

On the regular indie circuit, I was cocky. Full of myself sometimes. I performed with confidence because I knew I belonged right where I was.

Then I got a chance to go to IWA Mid-South in 2001.

When I walked into that locker room, everything changed. I was sitting with future superstars. CM Punk. Colt Cabana. Chris Hero. Dave Prazak. Jerry Lynn. Necro Butcher. Ian and Axl Rotten. B.J. Whitmer. Cash Flo. Corporal Robinson. Names that would go on to shape wrestling for the next two decades.

And suddenly that confidence disappeared.

Watching these guys perform live, delivering banger after banger, my self-belief hit an all-time low. Was I good enough? Did I belong here? These weren't questions I'd ever asked myself before. Now they were screaming in my head.

Then I found out my first matches were going to be against Ian Rotten. I'd watched Ian and Axl in ECW. I knew exactly what I was getting myself into. I was terrified I wasn't good enough to work with him, let alone survive in that environment.

When it was time for my debut, I made a choice.

I said "F*ck it. We're doing this." I lifted my head up high, took a deep breath, and "The Orient Express" Shank Dorscy took over.

Something strange happened in that match. Even though it was a hardcore weapons match and I bled everywhere, I was as calm as I'd ever been. I don't know why. I just was. We beat the crap out of each other.

While I was in the ring trying to recover from the loss, covered in blood, I heard Ian say to a fan as he walked back to the locker room: "That's a tough son of a bitch right there."

I never told anyone, but hearing that meant more to me than anyone realizes. It proved I could hang with those guys. It told me I belonged.

I never got to wrestle Punk, Colt, Hero, Jerry Lynn, B.J., or Necro. But I did get to work with Ian, Axl, Corp, Cash Flo, and others. And I appreciated every match and opportunity I was given while I was there.

The belief almost left me that day. But I chose to walk through the curtain anyway. And that choice changed everything.

When doubt creeps in, what choice are you going to make?

Choose to Believe

Belief is a choice.

You can choose to believe in yourself or you can choose to doubt yourself. You can feed the voice that builds you up or the voice that tears you down. You can carry yourself like you belong or like you're waiting for permission.

Nobody can make this choice for you. No trainer. No promoter. No mentor. It has to come from inside.

And it has to come before the proof. That's the hard part. You have to believe before you've made it. You have to feel like a star before anyone treats you like one.

But that's how it works. Belief comes first. Success follows.

Choose to believe. Every day. Even when it's hard. Even when the evidence isn't there yet.

Choose to believe and everything changes.

That's Law #2. Believe in yourself!

CHAPTER 5
LAW #3 – GET REALLY GOOD AT SOMETHING

Being good isn't good enough anymore.

There was a time when you could get by on just being a solid worker. Show up. Have a decent match. Go home. That was enough.

Those days are gone.

Today there are thousands of wrestlers. Thousands. All fighting for the same bookings. All trying to get noticed. All hoping to make it.

If you're just "good," you disappear into the crowd. You're one of a thousand good wrestlers that promoters scroll past. You're forgettable. You're replaceable.

Good doesn't get you booked. Good doesn't build a fanbase. Good doesn't make you money.

You have to be great at something.

Not great at everything. Nobody is great at everything. But great at something. One skill that makes you stand out. One ability that makes promoters pick up the phone. One quality that makes fans remember your name.

Your job is to find that specialty and get so good at it that nobody can ignore you.

The Myth of the Complete Wrestler

There's no such thing as a complete wrestler.

Every wrestler has strengths and weaknesses. Every single one. The greats included.

Hulk Hogan wasn't a great technical wrestler. Didn't matter. He was great at connecting with crowds and being larger than life.

Bret Hart wasn't a great talker. Didn't matter. He was great at telling stories in the ring and making everything look real.

Mick Foley wasn't a great athlete. Didn't matter. He was great at creating characters and making people feel something.

None of them were complete. They all had holes in their game. But they were so good at their specialty that nobody cared about what they couldn't do.

That's the lesson.

Stop trying to be complete. Stop trying to fix every weakness. Stop spreading yourself thin trying to be good at everything.

Pick your specialty. Get great at it. Let that greatness carry you.

What's Your Specialty?

It depends on you. On your type. On your natural strengths. On what comes easy to you.

Some wrestlers are great at promos. They can pick up a mic and make magic happen. Some are great at matches. They can work with anyone and have a banger every night. Some are great at characters, creating personas that people can't forget.

Others dominate with spots, doing things in the ring that make people's jaws drop. Some connect with crowds the second they walk through the curtain. Some are killers on social media, building audiences online and bringing fans to shows. And some wrestlers are great at the business side, understanding how wrestling makes money and helping promoters succeed.

Any of these can be yours. There's no right answer. The right answer is whatever fits you.

Look at your strengths. Look at what comes natural. Look at what you do better than most people without even trying.

That's probably where your answer lives.

The 3 Areas Every Wrestler Must Know

While you focus on getting great at one specialty, you can't be terrible at everything else. There are three areas every wrestler needs to know at least a little bit.

Wrestling. This is the basics. You have to be safe in the ring. You have to know how to work a match. You have to be able to go out there and not hurt yourself or your opponent. You don't have to be the best worker on the card. But you have to be competent. Promoters need to trust you in the ring. If they can't trust you, they won't book you.

Business. This is understanding how wrestling works as a business. How promoters make money. How bookings work. How to negotiate. How to be professional. How to be someone people want to work with. You don't have to be a business genius. But you have to understand the basics. Wrestlers who don't understand the business get taken advantage of. They make bad deals. They burn bridges without knowing it.

Media. This is everything outside the ring. Social media. Content creation. Building an audience. Getting yourself noticed online. You don't have to be a content machine. But you have to have some presence. Promoters look you up online before they book you. Fans find you through social media. If you don't exist online, you're invisible.

These three areas are the foundation. Wrestling. Business. Media.

You don't have to be great at all three. But you have to be solid enough that none of them kills your career.

Then you take one area and get great at it.

Why Promoters Book Who They Book

Being a promoter for over a decade, let me tell you how promoters think.

Promoters need to fill cards. They need to sell tickets. They need to put on shows that make money and make fans happy.

When a promoter is putting together a card, they're solving a puzzle. They need different pieces. Different types of wrestlers. Different skills.

They need someone who can work long matches. They need someone who can cut promos. They need someone who brings fans. They need someone who can work with green talent. They need someone who can do a high spot. They need someone who can be the monster heel. They need someone who can make people laugh.

Promoters aren't looking for good wrestlers. They're looking for wrestlers who solve problems.

If you're great at something, you solve a problem. You fill a slot on the card that needs to be filled. You become useful in a specific way.

If you're just good at everything, you don't solve any specific problem. You're a generic piece. Replaceable. Forgettable.

The wrestlers who get booked the most are the ones who are great at something specific. Promoters think of them when they need that skill.

"I need a comedy guy. Call him."

"I need someone who can go 30 minutes. Call her."

"I need a monster heel. Call him."

"I need someone with a following. Call her."

Be the person promoters call when they need something specific. That's how you stay booked.

Going Deep vs Going Wide

Most wrestlers go wide. They try to be good at everything. They spread their time and energy across a dozen skills.

The result? They're average at everything and great at nothing.

Smart wrestlers go deep. They pick one area and they pour everything into it. They become the best at that skill. Or at least one of the best.

Going deep means saying no to things that don't serve your focus. It means spending hours on your craft while other people spread themselves thin. It means being known for something specific.

This feels risky. What if you pick the wrong focus? What if you miss out by not developing other skills?

But the wrestlers who make it are almost always specialists. They're known for something. They have a clear identity.

The wrestlers who stay stuck are almost always generalists. They're decent at a lot of things. They're not known for anything.

Go deep. Not wide.

Pick your specialty. Pour yourself into it. Become undeniable at that one skill.

That's how you stand out.

The Danger of Being Well-Rounded

Being well-rounded can hurt your career.

I know that sounds wrong. We're taught that being well-rounded is good. That you should be balanced. That you should develop all your skills equally.

But in wrestling, well-rounded often means forgettable.

When a promoter is putting together a card, they don't think "I need a well-rounded wrestler." They think "I need someone who can do this specific skill really well."

Well-rounded wrestlers don't stand out. They don't fill a specific need. They're hard to describe in one sentence.

"What's that wrestler known for?"

"I don't know. He's pretty good at everything I guess."

That's the kiss of death. Pretty good at everything means not great at anything. And not great at anything means forgettable.

The wrestlers people remember are the specialists. The ones you can describe in one sentence.

"She's the best promo on the indies."

"He does spots nobody else will try."

"She's the funniest wrestler I've ever seen."

"He's a monster. Looks like he'll kill you."

One sentence. That's what you want. Be describable in one sentence because you're great at one skill.

When Good at Everything Means Great at Nothing

Shelton Benjamin might be the most athletic wrestler to never become a world champion.

Watch his matches. The guy could do things in the ring that defied physics. Remember when he ran up the ladder at WrestleMania? Remember his matches with Shawn Michaels? The man was a freak athlete. He could wrestle. He could sell. He had the look. He had the pedigree from training with Kurt Angle.

So why didn't Shelton become a main eventer?

Because nobody could describe him in one sentence.

Ask a wrestling fan to sum up Shelton Benjamin. They'll struggle. "He's really athletic" isn't a specialty. "He's a good wrestler" isn't a specialty. Those are generic descriptions that apply to hundreds of people.

Shelton was good at almost everything. He was great at nothing specific. He never found the one skill that made him undeniable. He never carved out an identity that made promoters say "we need Shelton for this."

He had a solid career. He's respected. He made money. But he should have been a world champion multiple times over. The talent was there. The identity wasn't.

Being good at everything kept him from being great at something. And great is what gets you to the top.

Can you describe yourself in one sentence? If you can't, that's a problem.

How to Pick Your Specialty

Some wrestlers struggle to pick a focus. They don't know what fits them.

Start with these questions.

Look at your strengths.

- What do you do better than most people?
- What comes easy to you?
- What do people compliment you on?

That's probably where your specialty lives.

Look at what you love.

- What part of wrestling gets you excited?
- What do you look forward to?
- What would you do even if nobody paid you?

You'll get great at things you love faster than things you force yourself to do.

Look at what's needed.

- What are promoters in your area looking for?
- What's missing from most cards?

- What can you provide that others can't?

Sometimes your specialty finds you because there's a gap to fill.

Look at what fits your type. Go back to Chapter 1.

- What's your wrestler personality type?
- What skills fit that type naturally?

A Powerhouse shouldn't try to be a high-flyer. A Performer shouldn't try to be a silent assassin. Pick something that matches who you are.

Try things and pay attention. Sometimes you don't know until you try. Experiment. Pay attention to what works and what doesn't. The crowd will tell you. The video will tell you. Your gut will tell you.

Your specialty might not be obvious right away. That's okay. Keep looking. Keep trying. Keep paying attention. You'll find it.

When One Skill Is Enough

Paul Heyman can't wrestle.

He's not athletic. He's not imposing. He's not going to have a five-star match with anyone. By every traditional measure of what a wrestler should be, Paul Heyman fails.

But Paul Heyman is one of the most successful people in wrestling history.

Because he found his specialty. And his specialty is talking.

Nobody cuts a promo like Paul Heyman. Nobody sells a match like Paul Heyman. Nobody makes you believe like Paul Heyman. When he picks up a microphone, you listen. Period.

He took that one skill and built an empire around it. He became the greatest manager of all time. He ran ECW. He's been the mouthpiece for Brock Lesnar, CM Punk, Roman Reigns. He made himself indispensable by being undeniably great at one specific skill.

Paul Heyman didn't waste time trying to become a better wrestler. He didn't spread himself thin learning skills he'd never master. He found his lane, went all in, and became the best in the world at it.

That's the lesson. You don't have to be good at everything. You have to be great at something. Find your lane and own it so completely that nobody can ignore you.

What's your specialty? And are you going all in on it?

The 10,000 Hour Reality

Getting great at something takes a long time.

You've probably heard of the 10,000 hour rule. It takes about 10,000 hours of practice to master something. That's years of work. Years of reps. Years of showing up day after day.

There are no shortcuts. There are no hacks. There's just the work.

Some wrestlers don't want to hear this. They want the quick fix. They want the secret that makes them great overnight.

There is no secret. There's just putting in the reps.

The wrestlers who become great at something are the ones who put in the time. They practiced when nobody was watching. They drilled the same skills over and over. They showed up day after day for years.

That's the price of greatness. Time and work. There's no other way.

If you're not willing to pay that price, you'll always be average. You'll always be forgettable.

But if you are willing to pay the price? If you're willing to put in the years and the reps and the work?

You can become undeniable.

Getting Better Every Day

Greatness doesn't happen all at once. It happens in small steps. Day by day. Rep by rep.

The goal isn't to be great tomorrow. The goal is to be a little better today than you were yesterday.

That's it. Just a little better. Every single day.

Those little improvements add up. Over weeks. Over months. Over years. One day you look up and you're not the same wrestler you were. You're great at something. You're undeniable.

But it happens so slowly you almost don't notice.

That's why most wrestlers quit. They want big results fast. They want to see progress in weeks, not years. They get frustrated when they're not great after six months.

Greatness doesn't work that way.

The wrestlers who make it are the ones who show up every day and get a little better. They trust the process. They know the reps will add up. They play the long game.

Get better every day. Even if it's just a little bit. That's how greatness is built.

Learning From Everyone

Great wrestlers learn from everyone. Not just from the legends. Not just from their trainers. From everyone.

Watch the wrestler who's been around forever. He might not be flashy but he knows how to pace a match, how to read a crowd, how to work safe.

Watch the young wrestler who just started. She might do something fresh. Something you never thought of. Something that sparks an idea.

Watch wrestlers outside your style. If you're a brawler, watch the technicians. If you're a technician, watch the high-flyers. You'll pick up things you can use.

Watch wrestlers in other promotions. Other countries. Other eras. There's wisdom everywhere if you're looking.

The wrestlers who get great are the ones who never stop learning. They stay curious. They stay humble. They know they don't know everything.

Be a student forever. Learn from everyone. That's how you keep getting better.

Keep Learning Forever

The wrestlers who last never stop learning.

Wrestling changes. What worked 10 years ago doesn't work today. What works today might not work in 10 years. The business evolves. The audience evolves. Technology evolves.

If you stop learning, you get left behind.

I've seen wrestlers peak in their 20s and fade in their 30s. Not because their bodies gave out. Because they stopped growing. They thought they had it figured out. They stopped learning.

And the business passed them by.

I've also seen wrestlers peak in their 40s. They stayed curious. They kept learning. They adapted to how the business changed. They stayed relevant.

The difference wasn't talent. It was mindset.

Never think you've arrived. Never think you know enough. Never stop being a student.

The moment you stop learning is the moment your career starts dying.

My Specialty Changed. Yours Can Too.

What I was known for has changed over the years. And that's okay.

When I was an active wrestler, I was known for hardcore matches. Blood. Weapons. Punishment. I was also known for being entertaining and funny. Those were my specialties back then.

But I wasn't known for being a businessman.

And that cost me everything.

When injuries forced me out of wrestling, I had nothing to fall back on. No savings. No nest egg. No backup plan. I had spent years building a reputation in the ring but zero time building income outside of it.

That was a hard lesson. One of the hardest I've ever learned.

When I came back to wrestling as a promoter with New Ohio Wrestling and as a trainer with NOW Elite Pro Wrestling Academy, I found a new focus. One I wish I had found twenty years earlier.

My specialty now is treating pro wrestling like a business.

I want to be known as the guy who teaches wrestlers how to build real income. Not just booking fees. Real income. Online income. Multiple streams. Money that doesn't disappear when your body breaks down.

The moment I realized what made me different was when I started thinking long-term. Most people in wrestling think about the next show. I started thinking about the next decade. What happens when you can't wrestle anymore? What happens when the bookings dry up? What happens when you're 40 and your body is done?

That's my lane now. Helping wrestlers build careers that don't leave them broke and broken when the ring life ends.

What's your specialty? And more importantly, will it still take care of you when you can't take bumps anymore?

Your Specialty Can Evolve

Your specialty doesn't have to stay the same forever.

When you start out, it might be one skill. As you grow, it might evolve into something else. Or you might add to it. Or you might find a new focus that fits better.

That's okay. That's growth.

The point isn't to lock yourself into one lane forever. The point is to have a clear identity right now. Something that makes you stand out. Something that gets you booked.

As you evolve, your specialty can evolve too. The comedian might become the comedy wrestler who can also work serious matches. The high-flyer might become the veteran who mentors young talent. The monster might become the promoter who builds the next generation.

Your specialty is your foundation. But foundations can be built on. They can expand. They can grow.

Start with one focus. Get great at it. Then see where it takes you.

Find Your Specialty and Own It

You need a specialty. Something you're great at. Something that makes you stand out. Something that makes promoters pick up the phone.

It doesn't matter what it is. Promos. Matches. Comedy. Characters. Spots. Social media. Business. Connections.

What matters is that you pick something and get great at it.

Go deep, not wide. Specialize, don't generalize. Be known for something, not nothing.

Know enough about wrestling, business, and media to not hurt your career. But pour your real energy into your specialty.

And never stop learning. Never stop growing. Stay a student forever.

That's Law #3. Get really good at something.

In a world of good wrestlers, the great ones get booked.

CHAPTER 6
LAW #4 – USE YOUR IMAGINATION

Everything happens twice.

First in your mind. Then in reality.

Every great match was imagined before it was wrestled. Every great promo was heard in someone's head before it was spoken. Every great character was seen in the mind before it walked through the curtain.

Nothing happens in wrestling that wasn't imagined first.

This is true for your career too. Before you can build something great, you have to see it. You have to picture it clearly in your mind. You have to know what it looks like, feels like, sounds like.

Most wrestlers never do this.

They show up and hope for the best. They take what comes. They react instead of create. They wait for someone else to imagine their future for them.

That's why most wrestlers stay stuck.

The ones who make it are the ones who see it first. They picture their future so clearly that it pulls them forward. They create in their minds before they create in reality.

Your imagination might be the most powerful tool you own. And almost nobody in wrestling is using it.

See It Before You Do It

This sounds strange but it's completely true.

Your brain doesn't know the difference between something you picture vividly and something you experience.

When you vividly picture doing something, your brain fires the same way it does when you actually do it. The same neurons. The same pathways. The same patterns.

This is why athletes visualize. They see themselves making the shot. Running the play. Winning the game. And their brain treats it like practice.

Wrestlers can do the same thing.

Picture your entrance. See the crowd. Hear the music. Feel your feet on the ramp. Watch yourself walk to the ring with confidence.

Picture your match. See the spots. Feel the timing. Watch yourself hit everything clean.

Picture your promo. Hear the words. Feel the emotion. Watch the crowd react.

When you do this, you're training your brain. You're building the pathways before you need them. You're making success familiar so it doesn't feel strange when it happens.

This isn't magic. It's how the brain works. Use it.

The Gimmick Starts in Your Head

Where do great gimmicks come from?

They come from imagination.

Every memorable character in wrestling history started as an idea in someone's head. Someone pictured a rattlesnake redneck who drinks beer and stuns his boss. Someone pictured a dead man who controls lightning. Someone pictured a narcissist who thinks he's the best looking person alive.

These ideas didn't fall from the sky. Someone created them. Someone used their mind.

Your gimmick has to start the same way.

Before you buy the gear. Before you pick the music. Before you cut the first promo. You have to see the character in your mind.

- Who is this person?
- What do they want?
- Why do they want it?
- How do they talk?
- How do they move?
- What makes them different from everyone else?

You have to picture this person so clearly that they feel real to you. You have to know them inside and out. You have to see them in your mind before anyone else can see them in the ring.

The more clearly you see your character, the more clearly you'll be able to play them. The more real they are in your head, the more real they'll be to the crowd.

Vision comes first. Everything else follows.

Going Deeper With Your Character

Most wrestlers picture their character on the surface. The look. The moves. The catchphrase.

But the best characters go deeper.

- What happened to this character before they became a wrestler?
- What's their backstory?
- What made them who they are?
- What does this character want more than anything?

Not just to win matches. What do they really want? Respect? Revenge? Money? Love? Power?

- What is this character afraid of?
- What's their weakness?
- What keeps them up at night?

- How does this character act when things go wrong?
- When they lose?
- When they get betrayed?
- When everything falls apart?

These questions might seem like overkill. You're not writing a novel. You're wrestling.

But when you know your character this deeply, everything becomes easier. You know how they'd react in any situation. You know what they'd say. You know how they'd move.

You stop playing a character. You become the character. And the crowd feels the difference.

Go deep. Don't just picture the surface. Picture the soul.

Building Your Gimmick Like a Business

Your gimmick isn't just a character. It's a business.

Your gimmick decides what merch you sell. What content you create. What fans you attract. What promoters book you. What money you make.

A good gimmick makes all of that easier. A bad gimmick makes it harder.

So when you're building your gimmick, think like a business owner.

Merch:

- Can this character sell merch?
- What would the t-shirt look like?
- What would the catchphrase be?
- Would fans want to wear this?

Content:

- Can this character create content?
- What would the social media look like?
- What kind of tapes would this character make?

- Would people follow them online?

Before you post a picture, think it through.

- Can this character get booked?
- What slot does this character fill on a card?
- Why would a promoter need this character?
- What problem does this character solve?

Longevity:

- Can this character make money long-term?
- Is this a gimmick that can last for years?
- Can it evolve?
- Will it still work when you're older?

These are business questions. And they matter.

A gimmick that's cool but can't sell merch is a problem. A gimmick that's funny but can't get booked is a problem. A gimmick that works now but can't evolve is a problem.

Use your creativity to build something that works as a business. Not just something that sounds cool.

Picture Your Future

One of the most powerful things you can do for your career is picture your future.

Not vaguely. Not "I want to be successful." Specifically. In detail. So clear you can taste it.

- Where are you wrestling five years from now?
- What does the building look like?
- How big is the crowd?
- What are they chanting?

- What's your character?
- What do you look like?
- What's your entrance like?

- How does the crowd react when your music hits?

- What's your life like outside wrestling?
- Where do you live?
- What's your income?
- What does your day look like?

See it. All of it. In as much detail as you can.

This isn't daydreaming. This is programming.

When you picture your future clearly, you give your brain a target. Your brain starts working toward that target even when you're not thinking about it. You start making decisions that move you toward that picture. You start noticing opportunities that fit.

Without a clear picture, your brain has nothing to aim at. You drift. You react. You go wherever the current takes you.

With a clear picture, you have direction. Purpose. A destination.

Picture your future. Make it so real in your mind that it feels like a memory from tomorrow.

Then go build it.

Working Backward

Once you can see your future clearly, you can work backward.

This is where vision becomes strategy.

Let's say you see yourself as a main event wrestler in five years. Okay. What does that person have that you don't have right now?

Maybe they have a bigger following. Okay.

- How do you build that?
- What do you need to do this year to grow your audience?

Maybe they have a better character. Okay.

- How do you develop that?

- What work do you need to do on your gimmick?

Maybe they have better relationships with promoters. Okay.

- How do you build those?
- Who do you need to meet?
- What bridges do you need to build?

You take the big picture and break it into smaller pieces.

- What has to happen in year four?
- Year three?
- Year two?
- Year one?
- This month?
- This week?

Working backward turns a dream into a plan. It connects where you are to where you want to be. It shows you the path.

Most wrestlers only think forward. They think about what they can do next. They take it one step at a time with no destination in mind.

Smart wrestlers think backward. They start with the end and figure out how to get there.

Vision shows you the destination. Working backward shows you the road.

When Talent Drifts Without Vision

Jeff Hardy is one of the most naturally gifted wrestlers to ever live.

Watch his matches. The guy could fly. He could connect with a crowd like few others. He had an aura that made people care about him the moment his music hit. Swanton Bombs off ladders. TLC matches that changed wrestling. A charisma that couldn't be taught.

But Jeff has been open about something. He never really had a plan.

He went where the wind took him. He reacted to whatever came next. He lived in the moment, which made him exciting to watch but also led to a career full of stops and starts. Suspensions. Releases. Returns. More suspensions. Opportunities that slipped away. Championships that could have been.

Jeff Hardy should have been THE guy for an entire era. He had everything. The look. The talent. The connection with fans. But without a clear vision of where he was going, he drifted. He's talked about his demons. He's talked about not thinking ahead. He's talked about just taking things as they came.

That's not a knock on Jeff. He's still a legend. But picture what could have been if that incredible talent had been paired with a clear vision. If he had seen his future and built toward it instead of just riding the wave.

Talent without vision drifts. Jeff Hardy is proof that even the most gifted wrestlers need more than ability. They need a picture of where they're going.

Do you have a clear picture? Or are you just going where the current takes you?

Before Every Match

You can start using this today.

Before every match, visualize.

See the match in your head before you go through the curtain. Picture the entrance. Picture the spots. Picture the finish. See yourself hitting everything clean.

Feel the emotions you want to feel. Confidence. Intensity. Focus. Whatever your character needs.

Hear the crowd. See their reactions. Picture them responding exactly the way you want.

This takes five minutes. Maybe less. But it changes everything.

When you've already seen the match in your head, you're not nervous. You're ready. You've already been there. Your brain knows what to do.

The best wrestlers do this before every match. It's part of their routine. They don't just prepare their bodies. They prepare their minds.

Start doing this. Before every match. Before every promo. Before every segment. See it first. Then do it.

Before Every Promo

Promos are where most wrestlers struggle. They freeze up. They forget their words. They sound scripted and fake.

Visualization can fix this.

Before you cut a promo, hear it in your head first. Not word for word. That's memorizing. This is different.

Hear the emotion. Feel what your character feels. See the reaction you want from the crowd.

- What does your character want to say?
- What do they need to get across?
- What emotion are they feeling?

When you've pictured the promo from the inside out, the words come easier. You're not reciting a script. You're expressing something you've already felt in your mind.

The best promos feel real because the wrestler felt them first. They lived the emotion before they spoke the words.

Feel it first. Then say it.

Content Starts in Your Head

In today's wrestling world, content matters.

Social media. YouTube. TikTok. Instagram. You need content to build reach. You need content to build your brand. You need content to stay visible.

And all that content starts in your head.

Before you shoot a tape, picture it.

- What's the concept?
- What's the hook?
- What makes someone stop scrolling?

Before you post a picture, think it through.

- What's the story?
- What does it say about your character?
- Why would someone care?

Before you create anything, see it in your mind.

The wrestlers who create great content are the ones with active minds. They're always thinking of ideas. Always seeing possibilities. Always picturing what could work.

The wrestlers who struggle with content are the ones who wait for ideas to come to them. They copy what others do. They post without thinking.

Your mind is a content machine if you let it be. Ideas are everywhere. You just have to train yourself to see them.

When something happens, ask yourself: Is there content in this?

When you have a thought, ask yourself: Would this make a good post?

When you see something that works for someone else, ask yourself: How could I do my version of this?

Keep your creativity active. Let it generate ideas constantly. Write them down before you forget them.

Content starts in your head. The more you use that muscle, the more content you'll create.

Capturing Your Ideas

Your brain will give you ideas at random times. In the shower. Driving to work. Lying in bed at night. In the middle of a conversation about something else.

Most people lose these ideas. They think "I'll remember that later." They don't. The idea disappears.

Don't let that happen.

Capture your ideas the moment you have them. Write them in your phone. Keep a notebook by your bed. Voice memo yourself while driving.

It doesn't matter how you capture them. What matters is that you do.

Most of your ideas won't be great. That's okay. You're not looking for perfect ideas. You're looking for raw material. Stuff you can work with later.

The more ideas you capture, the more you have to choose from. The best wrestlers and content creators have lists of ideas waiting to be used. They never run out because they never stop capturing.

Train yourself to capture ideas. Your brain is giving you gold. Don't let it slip away.

Visualization and Confidence

Nobody talks about this, but visualization builds confidence.

When you've pictured something a hundred times, it doesn't feel scary anymore. It feels familiar. You've already been there in your mind. You've already done it mentally.

Wrestlers who visualize their matches feel calmer in the ring. They've already seen it work. Their brain treats it like something they've done before.

Wrestlers who picture their promos feel more confident on the mic. They've already heard themselves nail it. Their brain knows it's possible.

Wrestlers who see their future clearly feel more certain about their path. They've already seen where they're going. Their brain believes it can happen.

Visualization doesn't just create your future. It prepares you for it emotionally. It makes success feel normal instead of surprising.

This is why champions visualize. Not because it's a nice idea. Because it works. It makes you ready for moments that would overwhelm someone who never pictured them.

When you get there, you'll feel like you've been there before.

Because you have. In your mind.

The Limits of Imagination

Imagination without action is just daydreaming.

You can picture your future all day long. You can visualize your matches in perfect detail. You can see your character down to the smallest detail.

But if you don't do the work, none of it matters.

Imagination is a tool. It's the first step. It shows you what's possible and prepares you to go get it.

But you still have to go get it.

You still have to train. You still have to take bookings. You still have to create content. You still have to build relationships. You still have to do the hard work every day.

Imagination without work is fantasy. Work without imagination is grinding in circles. You need both.

See it clearly in your mind. Then go make it real with your hands.

That's the formula.

When Vision Becomes Reality

Triple H saw the whole thing before it happened.

Not just being a wrestler. Not just being a champion. He saw himself running WWE.

A guy from New Hampshire pictured himself sitting in the chair that Vince McMahon built. And he spent decades making it real.

Every move Triple H made served that vision. He studied the business side while other wrestlers just focused on matches. He built relationships with the right people. He married into the family, sure, but he also made himself indispensable. He created NXT and proved he could develop talent. He positioned himself as the guy who understood both the creative and the corporate.

When other wrestlers were partying after shows, Triple H was learning how the business worked. When other wrestlers were focused on their next match, Triple H was thinking about the next decade. He saw a future where he ran the biggest wrestling company in the world, and he built toward it every single day.

Now look at where he is. Running WWE creative. Shaping the future of the entire industry. Living exactly the future he pictured.

That didn't happen by accident. That happened because he saw it first. He pictured it so clearly that every decision, every relationship, every move became a step toward that vision.

Triple H saw his future. Then he built it. That's the power of vision paired with execution.

What future are you picturing? And what are you doing today to build it?

Train Your Imagination

Imagination is a skill. You can get better at it.

Some people think creativity is something you're born with. You either have it or you don't.

That's not true. Imagination is like a muscle. The more you use it, the stronger it gets.

Start using yours.

Picture things on purpose. Visualize your matches before you have them. See your character in different situations. Picture your future in detail.

The more you do this, the easier it gets. The clearer the pictures become. The more ideas you generate.

Wrestlers who use their mind regularly have an advantage over wrestlers who don't. They see possibilities others miss. They create things others can't. They build futures others only dream about.

Your imagination is a gift. Don't waste it. Train it. Use it. Let it show you what's possible.

The Impossible Picture That Became Real

When I decided to go all in on New Ohio Wrestling, I knew I didn't want to be like other promotions.

I didn't just want to run shows in VFW halls and armories like everyone else. I wanted to do something that had never been done. Something that would put New Ohio Wrestling on the map. Something that would make the wrestling world take notice of what we are building in Columbus.

I started asking myself a question. What has an independent professional wrestling promotion never done? Not just in Columbus. Not just in Ohio. Anywhere in the world.

The answer hit me like a finishing move.

The Arnold Sports Festival.

The Arnold is the biggest multi-sport festival on the planet. Over 22,000 athletes. More than 80 sports and events. 200,000 fans descending on Columbus every year. Bodybuilding. Strongman.

Martial arts. Powerlifting. The biggest names in fitness walking those expo floors.

And in the entire history of the Arnold Sports Festival, no independent professional wrestling promotion had ever been part of it.

Not one. Ever. In the world.

I saw New Ohio Wrestling there. I saw it in my head before it existed. A wrestling ring in the middle of that expo. Our wrestlers performing in front of thousands of people who had never seen indie wrestling before. The NOW logo alongside all those world-class sports.

Everyone would have called me crazy. An indie promotion from Columbus thinking they belonged at the Arnold? With Arnold Schwarzenegger? Next to Olympic athletes and world champions?

But I saw it. And I started building toward it.

In 2018, we made our debut at the Arnold SportsWorld Kids & Teens Expo. We did it. The thing I pictured became real. New Ohio Wrestling became the first independent professional wrestling promotion to ever perform at the Arnold Sports Festival.

In 2019, we went back. And that's when something happened that I couldn't have pictured even in my wildest dreams.

We created the Arnold SportsWorld Kids & Teens Expo Championship. A four-man tournament to crown the first ever champion. The finals came down to "The Show" Robby Starr versus "Superman" Onyx.

During the championship match, the Terminator himself appeared out of nowhere.

Arnold Schwarzenegger. Walking to ringside. At our show. Doing a live social media recording for his millions of followers. Filming our match. Our wrestlers. Our promotion.

But it got better.

Robby Starr had been talking trash to Arnold during the match. After Onyx won, Starr tried to escape. Arnold wasn't having it. The Terminator himself rolled Robby Starr back into the ring. Right into the massive arms of our newly crowned champion.

Powerslam. Arnold cheering him on. The crowd going absolutely insane.

That moment made headlines. ComicBook.com covered it. Pro Wrestling Sheet picked it up. People around the world saw Arnold Schwarzenegger getting involved in a New Ohio Wrestling match.

You can't buy that. You can't plan that. But it happened because we were there. And we were there because I pictured it first.

Our third appearance was supposed to be at the 2020 Kids & Teens Expo. We had everything ready. The day before we were supposed to start setting up, the world shut down. COVID. The Kids & Teens Expo never returned.

But in 2022, we got another call.

This time it wasn't the Kids & Teens Expo. It was the main building. The Arnold Sports Festival itself. The big show. Three days straight of New Ohio Wrestling representing professional wrestling at the Arnold.

The Arnold Sports Festival has existed since 1989. Thirty-plus years of the biggest names in sports and fitness. And in all that time, no independent professional wrestling promotion had ever been considered good enough to represent pro wrestling at the Arnold.

We did it. Not once. Not twice. Three times.

No other indie promotion in the world can say that. Not in the history of the Arnold Sports Festival. We are the only ones.

That's something nobody can ever take away from us.

It started with vision. I saw New Ohio Wrestling at the Arnold before anyone else could see it. I pictured it so clearly that I built everything toward making it real.

What are you picturing right now? What's the thing that seems impossible? The goal everyone would call you crazy for wanting?

Picture it. See it clearly. Then start building.

That's the power of imagination.

Create Your Future

Your future is going to be created by someone's vision. Either yours or someone else's.

If you don't picture your future, you'll end up living in someone else's vision. You'll be a piece in their plan. A background player in their story.

But if you use your mind, you can create your own future. You can build your own vision. You can be the main character in your own story.

See it clearly. Picture every detail. See your character, your matches, your career, your life.

Then work backward. Figure out the steps. Make a plan.

Then execute. Do the work. Build what you pictured.

That's the formula. See it. Plan it. Execute it.

Everything happens twice. First in your mind. Then in reality.

What you picture today becomes what you live tomorrow.

So picture something great.

That's Law #4. Use your imagination.

CHAPTER 7
LAW #5 – MAKE A PLAN

Dreams without plans are just wishes.

Most wrestlers live like this. They have dreams. They have hopes. They have ideas about what they want to happen.

But they don't have a plan.

They wake up each day and react to whatever comes. They take bookings when they get offered. They post content when they feel like it. They work on their character when inspiration strikes.

And they wonder why nothing changes.

A dream without a plan is just a wish. You can wish all day long but wishing doesn't build careers. Planning does.

The wrestlers who make it are the ones who plan. They know what they're doing this week. This month. This quarter. This year. They're not reacting. They're executing.

It's time to become one of those wrestlers.

Why Plans Matter

A plan turns your mission into action. In Chapter 3, you picked your mission. You know where you're going. But knowing where you're going doesn't get you there. You need a map. You need steps. You need a plan.

A plan keeps you focused. Without one, everything feels urgent. Every opportunity looks good. Every distraction pulls at you. A plan tells you what matters and what doesn't. It keeps you on track.

A plan beats motivation. Motivation comes and goes. Some days you feel fired up. Some days you don't want to get out of bed. A plan doesn't care how you feel. It tells you what to do whether you're motivated or not.

A plan measures progress. Without one, you don't know if you're moving forward or running in circles. Milestones show you where you are and how far you've come.

A plan builds momentum. When you follow through and see results, you build confidence. That confidence builds more action. More action builds more results. It compounds over time.

Plans aren't sexy. Nobody posts about their planning sessions on social media. But plans are what separate the wrestlers who make it from the wrestlers who don't.

Why Most Wrestlers Don't Plan

If plans are so important, why don't most wrestlers have them?

A few reasons.

They think planning kills creativity. Some wrestlers believe that planning makes you rigid. That it boxes you in. That real artists just flow and let things happen. That's nonsense. Planning doesn't kill creativity. It channels it. It gives your creativity somewhere to go. The most creative people in any field are usually the most disciplined planners.

They don't know how to plan. Nobody teaches wrestlers how to plan. Wrestling school teaches you to bump and work and cut promos. It doesn't teach you to build a career. Most wrestlers have never been shown how to make a real plan.

They're afraid to commit. Making a plan means committing. It means saying "this is what I'm going to do." And that's scary. What if it doesn't work? What if they fail? So they stay vague. They keep their options open. They never commit to anything specific. And they never get anywhere.

They're too busy reacting. Some wrestlers are so caught up in day-to-day survival that they never step back to plan. They're always putting out fires. Always chasing the next booking. Always scrambling. They don't have time to plan because they don't have a plan. It's a trap that feeds itself.

The Cost of No Plan

Without a plan, you waste time. You spend hours on things that don't matter. You chase opportunities that lead nowhere. You work hard but not smart.

Without a plan, you miss opportunities. The best opportunities go to people who are ready for them. If you're never ready, they pass you by.

Without a plan, you stay stuck. You work for years and end up in the same place. You put in effort but don't see results. You keep doing the same things and expecting different outcomes.

Without a plan, you burn out. When you're reacting to everything, you're always stressed. Always overwhelmed. Always feeling behind. That wears you down. Eventually you quit because you're exhausted.

Without a plan, you build nothing. You don't build momentum. You don't stack wins. You don't create anything that lasts. You just survive from day to day.

I've seen talented wrestlers destroy their careers because they had no plan. All that talent. All that potential. Wasted because they never sat down and figured out what they were doing.

Don't let that be you.

When Talent Meets No Plan

Scott Hall might be the most naturally gifted wrestler who never reached his full potential.

Watch his work. The Razor Ramon character was money. His in-ring psychology was off the charts. His promos oozed cool. He had size, look, charisma, and talent that most wrestlers would kill for. He was one of the founding members of the nWo, which changed wrestling forever.

But Scott never had a plan.

He talked about it openly. He went where the money was. He reacted to whatever came next. He never sat down and mapped out where he wanted to be in five years or ten years. He just... went.

And we all know how that story played out. The demons. The substance issues. The stops and starts. The potential that was never fully realized. Hall himself admitted in interviews that he drifted through much of his career, making decisions based on the moment rather than any long-term vision.

Compare his career trajectory to guys with half his natural talent who built empires because they had a roadmap. Scott Hall should have been a multiple-time world champion. He should have been running a promotion or training the next generation at the peak of his powers. Instead, he spent years battling his own chaos.

That's not a knock on Scott. He's a legend. And thankfully, he found peace toward the end of his life thanks to DDP and others who helped him. But his career is a cautionary tale about what happens when incredible talent meets zero planning.

You can have all the gifts in the world. Without a roadmap, you're just drifting.

Do you have a plan? Or are you just taking whatever comes?

The 90-Day Plan

Time to get practical.

I want you to think in 90-day chunks.

Why 90 days?

Because it's long enough to make real progress but short enough to stay focused. A year feels too far away. A week feels too small. 90 days is the sweet spot.

Every 90 days, you should know exactly what you're working toward. What you want to accomplish. What actions you need to take. What milestones you're aiming for.

At the end of 90 days, you review. What worked? What didn't? What did you learn?

Then you map out the next 90 days.

This cycle keeps you moving forward. It keeps you learning. It keeps you adjusting.

Four 90-day cycles in a year. Four chances to set goals, work toward them, and review your progress. Four chances to get better at planning and executing.

In one year, you can transform your career if you use those four cycles well.

What Goes in a 90-Day Plan

Your 90-day plan should cover the key areas of your wrestling career.

Bookings.

- How many shows do you want to work this quarter?
- What promotions do you want to work for?
- What relationships do you need to build to make that happen?

Character development.

- What do you want to improve about your character?
- Your promos?
- Your in-ring work?
- Your look?

Pick one or two things to focus on.

Content and reach.

- What's your content plan?
- How many posts per week?
- What platforms are you focusing on?
- What's your goal for followers or engagement?

Skills.

- What skills are you developing?
- Are you training?
- Taking classes?
- Watching videos?
- Watching tapes?

Business.

- Are you building any income streams?
- Working on merch?
- Building an email list?
- Creating products?

Relationships.

- Who do you need to connect with?
- What promoters should you reach out to?
- What wrestlers should you build relationships with?

You don't have to go crazy on every area. Pick the ones that matter most right now. Set specific goals. Write down the actions you'll take.

That's your 90-day plan.

Don't just read this and nod your head.

That's what most wrestlers do. They read about planning. They agree with it. They feel motivated for about 20 minutes. Then they go back to reacting to whatever comes next.

I built a free 90-Day Wrestling Business Plan to make sure that doesn't happen to you. It covers all six areas. Bookings. Character. Content. Skills. Business. Relationships. You fill it out. You put it somewhere you'll see it. You work it.

This is the tool. Use it.

Download it free at **prowrestlingskool.com**

Then come back and keep reading. Because the plan is the big picture. The next section shows you what to do every single week to make it happen.

The Weekly Plan

90 days is the big picture. But you need a weekly plan too.

Every week, you should know what you're doing. Not vaguely. Specifically. What actions are you taking this week to move toward your 90-day goals?

This is where the real work happens. The 90-day plan tells you where you're going. The weekly plan tells you what to do right now.

At the start of each week, look at your 90-day goals.

- What needs to happen this week?
- What actions will move you forward?

Write them down. Put them on your calendar. Make them real.

At the end of each week, review.

- Did you do what you planned?
- What got in the way?
- What will you do differently next week?

This weekly rhythm keeps you accountable. It keeps you moving. It turns big goals into daily actions.

The Daily Habit

What are you doing every single day to build your career?

I'm not talking about big things. I'm talking about small habits. Things you do daily that add up over time.

Maybe it's 15 minutes of promo practice. Maybe it's posting one piece of content. Maybe it's reaching out to one person. Maybe it's watching one match and taking notes.

Small things. But done every day.

These daily habits compound. 15 minutes a day is over 90 hours a year. One post a day is 365 pieces of content. One connection a day is 365 new relationships.

The wrestlers who make it aren't always the ones who do big things. They're the ones who do small things consistently. Day after day. Week after week. Month after month.

Build daily habits that serve your mission. Small actions done consistently beat big actions done occasionally.

Your Content Schedule

In today's wrestling world, content is how you build reach. It's how fans find you. It's how promoters discover you. It's how you stay relevant between shows.

But most wrestlers post randomly. When they feel like it. When they remember. When inspiration strikes.

That doesn't work.

You need a content schedule. A roadmap for what you're posting and when.

This doesn't have to be complicated. Start simple.

How many times per week will you post? Pick a number you can actually hit. Three times? Five times? Every day? Be realistic.

What platforms will you focus on? You don't have to be everywhere. Pick one or two platforms and do them well.

What kind of content will you create? Behind the scenes? Training clips? Promos? Commentary? A mix?

When will you create and post? Block time on your calendar. Treat it like a booking. Don't skip it.

Having a schedule takes the guesswork out. You're not wondering what to post or when. You know. You just execute.

Batching Your Work

This tip will save you hours. Batch your work.

Batching means doing similar tasks all at once instead of spreading them throughout the week.

Instead of creating one piece of content each day, create seven pieces on Sunday. Instead of reaching out to one promoter at a time, reach out to ten in one session. Instead of editing videos one by one, edit them all in a batch.

Instead of creating one piece of content each day, create seven pieces on Sunday. Instead of reaching out to one promoter at a time, reach out to ten in one session. Instead of editing tapes one by one, edit them all in a batch.

Because switching between tasks costs time and energy. Every time you switch, your brain has to adjust. You lose focus. You lose momentum.

When you batch, you stay in one mode. You build momentum. You get more done in less time.

The wrestlers who create the most content usually batch it. They spend a few hours creating a week's worth of posts. Then they schedule them and focus on other things.

Find ways to batch your work. It changes everything.

Building Systems

Plans are good. Systems are better.

A plan tells you what to do. A system makes sure it gets done whether you're thinking about it or not.

What's the difference?

A plan says "I'm going to post three times this week."

A system says "Every Sunday at 10am, I create and schedule my content for the week. Every Monday, Wednesday, and Friday at noon, my posts go live automatically."

See the difference? The plan requires you to remember. The system runs on its own.

The more you can turn your plans into systems, the more consistent you'll be. You won't rely on motivation or memory. The system handles it.

Look at the areas of your career. Can you set up automatic posting? Can you create templates for reaching out to promoters? Can you build a routine for training that happens at the same time every week?

Systems take effort to set up. But once they're running, they free up your brain for other things.

When Planning Becomes a Career

Britt Baker planned her way to the top.

She went to dental school. Full dental school. While training to become a professional wrestler. While working the indie scene. While building a following.

That's not something you stumble into. That's a plan.

She knew she wanted to be a wrestler, but she also knew wrestling careers don't last forever. So she built a backup. She got her degree. She became a licensed dentist. She created a safety net that most wrestlers never think about.

Then she mapped out her wrestling career with the same precision.

She developed a character that stood out. “The D.M.D.” wasn’t just a nickname. It was a brand. It was merch. It was content. It was something promoters could sell. She built her promos around it. She built her social media around it. Everything connected.

When AEW launched, Britt wasn’t just another wrestler on the roster. She was a fully formed brand with a clear identity, a built-in story, and a strategy for how to get over. She became AEW Women’s Champion and one of the faces of the company.

None of that was luck. All of it was planning.

While other wrestlers were figuring it out as they went, Britt Baker had mapped out the whole thing. The dental career as a foundation. The character development. The brand building. The positioning.

That’s what planning looks like. And that’s why Britt Baker is where she is today.

What’s your plan? Is it as clear as hers?

When Plans Fall Apart

Plans don’t always work.

Life gets in the way. Shows get canceled. You get hurt. Opportunities come up that you didn’t expect. Things happen.

That’s okay. Plans aren’t meant to be perfect. They’re meant to be useful.

When your plan falls apart, don’t throw it away. Adjust it.

Look at what happened. What changed? What do you need to do differently? Update your plan and keep moving.

The goal isn't to follow the plan perfectly. The goal is to have direction. To keep moving forward. To learn and adjust as you go.

Flexible plans beat rigid plans. And any plan beats no plan.

Planning Is a Skill

Planning is a skill. And like any skill, you get better at it with practice.

Your first few plans might not be great. You might set goals that are too big or too small. You might miss important areas. You might not know what actions to take.

That's okay. You'll learn.

Every 90 days, you'll get better at planning. You'll learn what works for you. You'll get more realistic about what you can accomplish. You'll get better at breaking big goals into small actions.

Don't wait until you know how to make a perfect plan. Make an imperfect one now. Learn from it. Make a better one next time.

The wrestlers who win aren't the ones who make perfect plans. They're the ones who make plans at all.

A Through Z and 1, 2, 3

I'm going to be honest with you.

In my personal life, I'm a terrible planner. Total chaos. If it wasn't for my wife Terrie, I'd probably forget to pay bills, miss appointments, and live in complete disorder. She keeps my life running. I'm not ashamed to admit that.

But when it comes to booking a show for New Ohio Wrestling? My planning is meticulous.

Most fans don't realize how complicated running a pro wrestling event is. There are a hundred moving pieces. Talent. Travel.

Lodging. Ring setup. Sound. Lighting. Merch. Tickets. Marketing. Timing. Storylines. Match order. Safety. Communication. Contingency plans for when things go wrong.

My good friend "Big" Tom Williams of WAR Wrestling told me something years ago that always stuck with me. He said when you create a pro wrestling event, you have to plan for A through Z and 1, 2, 3.

He was absolutely right.

It's way too much for one person to handle without a system. Most people would drown in it. I've seen promoters drown in it.

So I built a framework.

Every event follows the same planning structure. Every show gets the same checklist. Every detail gets tracked the same way. It's not sexy. It's not creative. It's a boring system that makes sure nothing falls through the cracks.

You want to know how well it works?

At the Arnold Sports Festival, I was responsible for close to 120 wrestlers and staff over a three-day weekend. Three days of live professional wrestling at one of the biggest sports expos in the world. Hundreds of moving pieces. Countless opportunities for disaster.

I can count on one hand the number of mistakes or things I forgot across all three times we did the Arnold.

Not because I'm a genius. I'm not.

Because I had a plan. A framework. A system that ran whether I was stressed or tired or overwhelmed.

That framework is the difference between pulling off a massive event and having it fall apart in your hands.

You don't need to be the smartest person in the room. You don't need to have everything figured out. You just need a plan and the discipline to follow it.

What's your framework? What's your system? Or are you just winging it and hoping for the best?

Start Now

You need a plan.

Not a vague idea of what you want. Not hopes and dreams. A real plan with real goals and real actions.

Start with 90 days. What do you want to accomplish? What areas will you focus on? What actions will you take?

Then break it into weeks. What are you doing each week to hit those goals?

Then build daily habits. Small actions done consistently that add up over time.

Create a content schedule. Batch your work. Build systems that run without you.

When things fall apart, adjust and keep moving. Learn from what works and what doesn't. Get better at planning every quarter.

This isn't sexy. This isn't exciting. This is the boring work that builds careers.

But boring works. Plans work. And the wrestlers who plan are the wrestlers who win.

That's Law #5. Make a plan.

Your future won't build itself. Plan it. Then build it.

CHAPTER 8
LAW #6 – MAKE DECISIONS FAST

Indecision is a career killer.

I've watched more wrestlers destroy their careers by not deciding than by deciding wrong. They sit on the fence. They wait for the perfect moment. They gather more information. They ask more people for advice.

And while they're thinking, opportunities pass them by.

The wrestling business moves fast. Opportunities come and go. Promoters need answers now. Fans move on quickly. The window opens and closes before most wrestlers even notice it was there.

The wrestlers who make it are the ones who decide fast. They see an opportunity, they make a call, they move. They don't get paralyzed by options. They don't wait for certainty that never comes.

Speed wins. In wrestling and in life. It's time to become a faster decision maker.

The Cost of Indecision

Lost opportunities.

A promoter calls with a last-minute booking. You hesitate. You want to think about it. By the time you decide, they've called someone else. Opportunity gone.

A chance to cut a promo opens up at a show. You're not sure if you should take it. You overthink it. Someone else steps up. Opportunity gone.

A wrestler wants to work with you on content. You're not sure if it's worth your time. You don't respond for a week. They've moved on. Opportunity gone.

Every time you hesitate, you risk losing something you can't get back.

Lost momentum.

Momentum in wrestling is everything. When things are moving, you need to keep them moving. When you stop to overthink, momentum dies.

I've seen wrestlers get hot, then stall because they couldn't decide what to do next. They had options. They had opportunities. But they couldn't pick one. So they picked none. And the heat went away.

Lost respect.

Promoters don't like dealing with wrestlers who can't make decisions. They need people who can give them a yes or no. People they can count on to commit.

When you're wishy-washy, promoters stop calling. They go to wrestlers who make their job easier. Wrestlers who decide.

Lost confidence.

Every time you don't decide, you train yourself to be indecisive. You reinforce the habit. You become the person who can't commit.

And that lack of confidence shows. In how you wrestle. In how you cut promos. In how you carry yourself. The crowd can feel when someone doesn't trust themselves.

Indecision is expensive. It costs you opportunities, momentum, respect, and confidence. And you often don't realize you're paying the price until it's too late.

Why Wrestlers Struggle to Decide

If indecision is so costly, why do wrestlers struggle with it?

Fear of being wrong. This is the big one. Most people don't decide because they're scared of making the wrong choice. They think if they wait long enough, the right answer will become obvious. But there's rarely a clearly right answer. Most choices are between good options with different tradeoffs. Waiting doesn't make the answer clearer. It just delays the decision.

Too many options. Sometimes wrestlers have too many choices. Which promotion to work for. Which character to develop. Which platform to focus on. Which opportunity to chase. More options feels like freedom. But too many options leads to paralysis. You can't pick because you can't compare everything. So you pick nothing.

Fear of missing out. When you commit to one path, you're saying no to other paths. That feels like loss. You might miss something better. You might regret your choice. So you keep your options open. You don't commit. You stay in limbo. And you miss everything because you couldn't commit to anything.

Waiting for permission. Some wrestlers don't decide because they're waiting for someone to tell them what to do. A trainer. A promoter. A mentor. They want validation before they commit. But nobody is coming to make your decisions for you. Your career is yours. Your choices are yours. Waiting for permission is just another form of not deciding.

And if you are 100% dead set on waiting for permission then I, right here and now, give you whatever permission you need to decide. Make the decision and move on.

Perfectionism. Some wrestlers want to make the perfect decision. They gather all the information. They analyze every angle. They try to eliminate all risk. But perfect decisions don't exist. Every choice has risk. Every option has downsides. If you're waiting for the perfect choice, you'll wait forever.

The Truth About Decisions

This might free you.

Most decisions are reversible.

You try a gimmick and it doesn't work. You can change it. You commit to a platform and it's not right for you. You can switch. You take a booking that turns out badly. You don't have to go back.

We treat decisions like they're permanent. Like one wrong choice will ruin everything. But most choices aren't like that. You can adjust. You can course correct. You can try again.

The cost of deciding wrong is usually smaller than the cost of not deciding at all.

Another truth: *you can't know the outcome in advance.*

No matter how much you think about it, you can't predict the future. You won't know if a decision was right until you make it and see what happens.

Waiting for certainty is pointless. Certainty doesn't exist. You have to decide with incomplete information and figure out the rest as you go.

And one more: *action creates clarity.*

When you're stuck between options, more thinking rarely helps. But action does. Make a choice, take action, and suddenly things become clearer. You learn things you couldn't learn by thinking.

The clarity you're looking for comes from doing, not deliberating.

When Indecision Kills a Career

WWE gave Ryback every opportunity.

The look. The intensity. The crowd reaction. When he was on that "Feed Me More" run, the fans were eating out of his hand. He was getting booked like a monster. He had main event matches. He had a world title shot against CM Punk. The machine was behind him.

But Ryback couldn't decide what he wanted to be.

He wanted to be pushed like a top guy, but he complained publicly when the booking didn't go his way. He wanted to be a team player, but he aired grievances that made the locker room uncomfortable. He wanted creative freedom, but he clashed with the people who controlled creative. He wanted to stay, but he kept threatening to leave.

One foot in, one foot out. Never fully committed to any direction.

The result? WWE stopped investing in him. Why push someone who might turn on you at any moment? Why build a storyline around someone who can't commit? Ryback went from potential main eventer to released, and his post-WWE career never gained traction because the same pattern continued.

Compare him to guys with less natural ability who committed fully and built long careers. Ryback had the tools. He just couldn't decide how to use them.

Indecision didn't just slow his career. It ended it before it really got started.

Are you fully committed? Or do you have one foot out the door?

The Big Decisions Wrestlers Face

Some specific decisions trip wrestlers up over and over.

Babyface or heel? This one paralyzes people. They see benefits to both. They don't want to limit themselves. So they stay in the middle, which is the worst place to be. Pick one. Commit to it fully. You can always turn later. But right now, be something specific. Wishy-washy characters don't get over.

Stay indie or try to get signed? Some wrestlers agonize over this for years. They don't know which path to pursue. So they half-pursue both and fully pursue neither. Make a choice. If you want to stay indie and build your own brand, commit to that. If you want to get signed, focus everything on that goal. Half measures lead to half results.

This promotion or that promotion? When you have options, it's tempting to keep all of them open. But that divides your focus. That splits your loyalty. That prevents you from building deep relationships anywhere. Pick the promotion that fits your mission best. Commit to them. Be their guy. You can always expand later. But right now, go deep instead of wide.

Social media or in-ring? Some wrestlers can't decide where to put their energy. Should they focus on getting better in the ring? Or should they focus on building an online audience? The answer is usually both, but one should be primary. Make that decision. Is this the season for developing your skills? Or is this the season for building your platform? Pick one to lead. The other supports it.

Keep your day job or go full-time? This is a big one. And it should be made carefully. But I've seen wrestlers sit on this decision for years, never committing to either path. If you're keeping your day job, commit to that and build wrestling around it without guilt. If you're going full-time, make a plan and make the leap. The middle ground of constantly wondering is exhausting.

How to Decide Faster

You can train yourself to decide faster. These tools help.

Set a deadline. Open-ended decisions drag on forever. Give yourself a deadline. "I will decide by Friday." "I will decide in 24 hours." "I will decide before I leave this room." Deadlines force action. Without them, you'll keep putting the decision off.

Limit your options. More options make decisions harder. Before you decide, narrow your choices. Cross off the options that clearly aren't as good. Get down to two or three real contenders. It's much easier to choose between two things than between ten.

Use your mission as a filter. Remember your mission from Chapter 3? Use it as a decision-making tool. Which option moves you toward your mission? Which one pulls you away? Let your mission decide for you.

Trust your gut. You know more than you think you know. Your gut has processed information your conscious mind hasn't caught up with yet. When you've thought about something for a while and you still can't decide logically, trust your gut. It's often right.

Ask: *What's the worst case*? For most decisions, the worst case isn't that bad. You can recover. You can adjust. You can try again. When you realize the downside is survivable, deciding becomes less scary.

Ask: *What would I tell a friend*? If a friend came to you with this exact decision, what would you tell them? Often we can see clearly for others what we can't see for ourselves. Take your own advice.

Flip a coin. This sounds stupid but it works. When you truly can't decide, flip a coin. Not to let the coin decide. But to notice how you feel when you see the result. If the coin says A and you feel disappointed, you wanted B. If the coin says A and you feel relieved, you wanted A. The coin reveals what you actually want.

Commit Completely

Making a decision is only half the battle. The other half is committing to it.

A half-hearted decision is barely better than no decision. When you decide but don't commit, you sabotage yourself. You do the thing, but you're always wondering if you should have done something else. You never give it your full effort.

That guarantees failure.

When you make a decision, burn the boats. Go all in. Stop looking at other options. Stop wondering if you made the right choice. Commit completely and make it work.

This is how good decisions become great results. Not because the decision was perfect. But because the commitment was total.

I've seen wrestlers make questionable decisions and succeed because they committed fully. I've seen wrestlers make smart decisions and fail because they kept second-guessing.

Commitment beats cleverness. Every time.

When Fast Decisions Build Empires

MJF decided exactly who he was going to be, and he never wavered.

From the moment he showed up, Maxwell Jacob Friedman knew his character. Arrogant. Hateable. The guy you pay money to see get beat up. He didn't test different gimmicks. He didn't try being a babyface first. He didn't ask permission or wait for someone to tell him what to do.

He decided. Then he committed completely.

Every promo. Every match. Every social media post. Every interview. All of it served the same character. No breaks. No winking at the camera. No hedging his bets in case it didn't work.

And it worked.

MJF became one of the biggest stars in wrestling by his mid-twenties. He's held world championships. He's main evented major shows. He's made himself so valuable that companies fight over him.

None of that happened because MJF was the most athletic or the most technically skilled. It happened because he decided fast, committed fully, and never looked back.

While other wrestlers were still figuring out their gimmick, MJF was building an empire around his. While others were testing the waters, he was all in.

That's the power of fast decisions and total commitment.

What have you decided about your character? Your brand? Your career? And are you all in?

What If You Decide Wrong?

You will decide wrong sometimes. Everyone does.

So what?

A wrong decision that you make quickly, learn from quickly, and correct quickly is better than no decision at all.

When you realize you've decided wrong, don't beat yourself up. Don't dwell on it. Learn the lesson and make a new decision.

"That gimmick didn't work. I learned why. Now I'm trying this."

"That promotion wasn't the right fit. I learned what I needed. Now I'm going here."

"That content strategy failed. I learned what doesn't work. Now I'm doing this."

Mistakes are data. They tell you something. Use them and move forward.

The wrestlers who make it aren't the ones who never make wrong decisions. They're the ones who make decisions quickly, learn quickly, and adjust quickly.

Speed beats perfection.

Decision Fatigue Is Real

Decision fatigue is real. The more decisions you make, the harder each decision becomes. Your brain gets tired.

This is why successful people often simplify their lives. They eat the same things. They wear the same clothes. They build routines. They eliminate small decisions so they have energy for big ones.

Look at your life. Where are you spending decision energy on things that don't matter? Can you simplify? Can you build systems that decide for you?

Save your decision energy for the choices that actually matter. Don't waste it on what to eat for breakfast or what to post today. Systematize the small stuff so you can focus on the big stuff.

The Decision That Changed My Life

The decision that changed my life happened because my wife told me to get the wrestling ring out of our garage.

Back up a little.

During COVID, indie wrestling basically shut down. My day job had me working from home as non-essential. I had a lot of time to think. And one thing kept coming up in my head.

I was getting older. My parents had struggled with health issues and passed away earlier than they should have. That scared me. I had type 2 diabetes. I was 308 pounds at my heaviest. The math wasn't good.

In 2021, things started opening back up. I was talking with my friend Shawn Jones, who wrestles as "Superman" Onyx, about my weight. He was a personal trainer with his own studio. He told me to stop by sometime and he'd give me a free workout to see where I was physically.

Sounded fun. So I went.

Thank God nobody else was there that day. Because I completely humiliated myself.

I couldn't do a situp. I couldn't do a pushup. This man was one of my wrestlers. Someone I hired. A good friend. And I went to his fitness studio and made a total ass out of myself.

I was embarrassed. But that embarrassment lit a fire.

Around the same time, something else happened. My wife Terrie has told me many times that I'm a little hard to live with when I get antsy and have a lot of pent-up energy. One day I must have gotten on her last nerve because she told me I needed to get our wrestling ring out of the garage, find a place to set it up, and blow off some steam.

Big Dirty, our wrestling ring, had been sitting in the garage since the pandemic shut everything down. What she said made perfect sense.

I made the decision immediately. Find a spot for the ring.

I found a space that barely fit the ring and a couple chairs. It was a start. Then I started thinking about a workout I could do in the ring that would help me get in shape so I didn't humiliate myself again like I did at Shawn's studio.

The more I thought about it, the more a vision started forming. A fitness program that was fun. That anyone could do. That used a pro wrestling ring to make it interesting.

That's where WrestleFit was born.

I wasn't anywhere close to being a personal fitness trainer. So I took my idea to Shawn to see if he wanted to partner up and create the program together. He loved it. He agreed. WrestleFit was created, and I was the first client.

We moved Big Dirty into a bigger facility. We added the fitness equipment we needed. We built the program.

Since starting WrestleFit, I went from 308 pounds at my heaviest down to 225 pounds. I can do situps now. I can do pushups. I can do things I never thought possible when I was gasping for air on Shawn's studio floor.

That quick decision to take Terrie's advice and find a spot for the wrestling ring changed my physical health. It changed my mental health. It might have even saved my life.

All because I decided fast and moved.

What decision are you sitting on right now that could change everything?

Decide and Move

You need to decide faster.

Stop waiting for certainty. It's not coming. Stop waiting for the perfect option. It doesn't exist. Stop waiting for permission. Nobody's going to give it to you.

Make decisions quickly. Trust yourself. Commit completely.

When you're wrong, learn and decide again. When you're right, build on it.

The wrestling business rewards speed. The wrestlers who decide fast get the opportunities. The wrestlers who wait get left behind.

That's Law #6. Make decisions fast.

Your career won't wait for you to make up your mind. Decide and move.

CHAPTER 9
LAW #7 – NEVER QUIT

Most wrestlers quit.

Not all at once. Not in a dramatic moment. They fade. They slow down. They stop showing up. They let the dream die one missed booking at a time.

I've seen it happen more times than I can count. Talented wrestlers with potential. Wrestlers who could have made it. Wrestlers who were closer than they realized.

They quit.

I know. Because I was one.

And the ones who stayed? The ones who kept showing up when it was hard? They got the spots the quitters left behind.

This business is brutal. It will test you. It will break you down. It will make you question everything. The ones who survive aren't always the most talented. They're the ones who refused to walk away.

You need to become one of those wrestlers.

Why Wrestlers Quit

Before we talk about not quitting, let's understand why people walk away in the first place.

The money isn't there. This is the big one. Wrestling doesn't pay well at the beginning. Sometimes it doesn't pay at all. You're spending money on gear, training, food, and travel while getting almost nothing back. That's hard. Bills pile up. Life gets expensive.

At some point, many wrestlers look at the math and decide it doesn't add up.

The progress feels slow. You work hard. You train. You take bumps. You drive hours to shows. And for what? You're still on the bottom of the card. You're still getting paid nothing. You're still not where you want to be. When progress feels slow, motivation dies. You start wondering if you're wasting your time. You start thinking maybe you're not good enough.

The rejection piles up. Promoters don't call you back. You don't get the booking. Someone else gets the push. You get passed over again and again. Rejection hurts. And when it keeps happening, it wears you down. You start to believe what the rejection is telling you. That you're not good enough. That you don't belong.

Life gets in the way. Relationships. Kids. Jobs. Health problems. Family emergencies. Life doesn't stop because you want to wrestle. Sometimes the stuff outside wrestling makes it impossible to keep going. The dream gets pushed aside for survival. Which is what happened to me.

The love fades. This one's painful. Some wrestlers fall out of love with wrestling. The thing that used to light them up starts to feel like a chore. The passion dies. When you don't love it anymore, it's hard to keep sacrificing for it.

The Quitting Point

Most wrestlers walk away at the same point.

It's not at the very beginning, when everything is new and exciting. It's not after they've made it, when the rewards are flowing.

It's in the middle.

It's after they've been around long enough to know how hard it is. After the excitement wears off. After they've been rejected enough times to start doubting themselves.

It's in the grind. The long stretch where progress is slow and rewards are few. The part where you have to keep going on faith because the results aren't showing yet.

That's where most wrestlers walk away.

And many of them do it right before things would have turned around. They were closer than they knew. A few more months. A few more shows. A few more connections.

But they couldn't see it. All they could see was the struggle. So they stopped.

Don't let that be you.

The Truth About Success Timelines

Success takes longer than you think.

We see successful wrestlers and we see where they are now. We don't see the years of struggle that got them there. We don't see the bad shows. The empty crowds. The times they wanted to give up.

We see the highlight reel. We don't see the behind-the-scenes.

This gives us unrealistic expectations. We think we should be further along by now. We think success should have happened already. We compare our beginning to someone else's middle.

That's a trap.

Success in wrestling usually takes years. Not months. Years. Years of showing up. Years of getting better. Years of building relationships. Years of paying dues.

If you're expecting fast results, you're going to be disappointed. And that disappointment will make you want to walk away.

Adjust your timeline. Give yourself permission to take longer. Understand that the struggle is part of the process, not a sign that you're failing.

When Walking Away Becomes a Pattern

Low Ki might be the most talented wrestler to never reach his full potential.

Watch his matches. The guy was special. Stiff kicks that looked like murder. Intensity that jumped off the screen. Technical ability that put him in conversations with the best in the world. He was one of the first Ring of Honor champions. He was in the first match in TNA history. He had runs in WWE developmental, NJPW, Impact, and basically every major promotion on the planet.

But Low Ki kept walking away.

He'd get opportunities, then burn bridges. He'd build momentum, then leave. He'd get close to a breakthrough, then something would happen and he'd be gone. Over and over again.

By all accounts, the issues were usually about creative differences, money disputes, or clashing with management. Maybe he was right in those situations. Maybe he wasn't. But the pattern was undeniable. Low Ki couldn't stay anywhere long enough to reach the heights his talent deserved.

Compare him to wrestlers with half his ability who stayed put, built relationships, and rode opportunities to the top. Low Ki had the talent to be a legitimate main eventer anywhere in the world. Instead, he became a cautionary tale about what happens when you keep leaving before the payoff comes.

Talent means nothing if you're not there when your moment arrives.

Are you building something? Or are you looking for the exit?

Rejection Is Part of the Game

If you're going to wrestle, you're going to get rejected. A lot. It's built into the business.

You'll reach out to promoters who never respond. You'll apply for spots you don't get. You'll watch other wrestlers get opportunities you wanted. You'll hear no more than you hear yes.

That's normal. That's the business. That's what everyone goes through.

The problem is when you take rejection personally. When you let it mean something about you. When you let it pile up inside until you can't take anymore.

Rejection doesn't mean you're not good enough. It means that particular opportunity wasn't the right fit at that particular time. That's all.

The most successful wrestlers in history got rejected constantly. They just didn't let it stop them. They kept going. They found the opportunities that were right for them.

Rejection is information. It tells you something didn't work. It doesn't tell you to give up. It tells you to try something different.

Dealing With Bad Shows

Bad shows happen.

The crowd is dead. Your match doesn't click. You botch something important. The whole night feels like a disaster.

When you're driving home from a bad show, walking away feels reasonable. You replay every mistake. You wonder why you're doing this. You feel embarrassed and frustrated.

This is when a lot of wrestlers tap out. Not in the moment. But they start pulling back. They book fewer shows. They stop trying as hard. The bad show becomes the beginning of the end.

Don't let one bad show define you.

Every wrestler has bad shows. Every single one. The greats have bombed. The legends have had nights they want to forget. It's part of the deal.

What separates the ones who make it from the ones who don't? They come back. They show up for the next one. They learn what they can and move forward.

A bad show is just data. It tells you something. Maybe you need more reps. Maybe that spot doesn't work. Maybe you were tired or unprepared.

Take the lesson. Leave the shame. Show up for the next one.

Dealing With Haters

The longer you're in wrestling, the more haters you'll collect.

Online trolls who criticize everything you do. Other wrestlers who talk behind your back. Fans who decide they don't like you. People who want to see you fail.

Haters come with the territory. If you're doing anything worth noticing, someone will hate you for it.

Some wrestlers let haters destroy them. They read every negative comment. They obsess over what people say. They let the criticism into their head until it poisons everything.

That's a path to walking away.

You have to learn to let it go. Not every opinion matters. Not every criticism is valid. Not every voice deserves space in your head.

Focus on the people who support you. Focus on getting better. Focus on your mission.

The haters are background noise. They don't get to decide if you stop. Only you get to decide that.

Small Wins Add Up

When progress feels slow, it's because you're looking for big wins.

The big booking. The big push. The big moment. The thing that changes everything overnight.

Big wins are rare. Most careers aren't built on big wins. They're built on small wins that add up over time.

You had a good match. Small win.

A fan asked for a picture. Small win.

A promoter said you did solid work. Small win.

Your social media grew a little. Small win.

You learned something new. Small win.

These don't feel like much in the moment. But they stack. Over months and years, small wins compound into something real.

The wrestlers who walk away are often the ones who only count big wins. They dismiss the small stuff. They don't see the progress because they're looking for the wrong thing.

Start counting your small wins. Write them down if you have to. Train yourself to notice progress even when it's incremental.

Small wins are proof that you're moving forward. They're fuel to keep going. They're evidence that stopping would be a mistake.

The Compound Effect

Success doesn't move in a straight line. It moves in a curve.

In the beginning, you put in a lot of effort and see very little result. You work hard and nothing seems to change. This is where most people give up.

But if you keep going, something shifts. The effort starts to compound. The skills you built start combining. The relationships you made start paying off. The content you created starts getting noticed.

Progress that was invisible becomes visible. Results that were slow become fast. Suddenly things are happening. Suddenly it looks like overnight success.

But it wasn't overnight. It was years of compounding. Years of small wins stacking up. Years of refusing to stop when it felt pointless.

The wrestlers who make it understand this. They know the slow part comes before the fast part. They know you have to survive the compound curve before you get the compound results.

Keep going. The curve is coming.

The Outlast Strategy

This strategy works every time: outlast everyone.

Most of your competition will walk away. They'll get tired. They'll get frustrated. They'll move on to something else. They'll decide wrestling isn't worth it.

If you just keep going, you'll end up with less competition. Opportunities that went to others will come to you. Spots that were crowded will open up.

This isn't a sexy strategy. It's not about being the best or the most talented. It's about being the last one standing.

I've seen average wrestlers build great careers simply by not walking away. They outlasted the talented people who gave up. They were there when opportunities came because everyone else had left.

You don't have to beat everyone. You just have to outlast them.

Keep showing up. Keep getting better. Keep building relationships. And watch as the people around you slowly disappear.

The ones who stay win.

When Refusing to Quit Changes Everything

Diamond Dallas Page didn't start wrestling until he was 35 years old.

Let that sink in. Most wrestlers are hitting their prime at 35. DDP was just getting started. He'd been a manager. He'd been around the business. But as an in-ring performer? He was a complete beginner at an age when most people would say it's too late.

Everyone told him he couldn't do it. Too old. Too green. No athletic background. He'd never make it.

DDP didn't stop.

He trained harder than anyone. He studied tape obsessively. He worked on his weaknesses relentlessly. He got better slowly, painfully, year after year.

The rejection was constant. WCW kept him in the midcard for years. He wasn't seen as a real main eventer. He was the guy who worked hard but would never be "the guy."

DDP didn't stop.

At 43 years old, Diamond Dallas Page became WCW World Heavyweight Champion. Forty-three. An age when most wrestlers are retired or broken down. He main evented pay-per-views. He had classic matches. He became one of the most beloved wrestlers of his era.

And he's still not done. After wrestling, he created DDP Yoga and helped save the lives of wrestlers like Jake Roberts and Scott Hall. He built a whole second career out of refusing to stop.

None of that happens if DDP listens to the people who told him he was too old. None of that happens if he gives up when progress is slow. None of that happens if he walks away when the rejection piles up.

DDP refused to stop. And it changed everything.

What's your excuse again?

When Quitting Is Right

I need to be honest about something.

Sometimes walking away is the right choice.

If wrestling is destroying your health and you can't do it safely anymore, stepping back might be right.

If wrestling is destroying your family and you've done everything you can to balance it, stepping back might be right.

If you've genuinely fallen out of love with wrestling and it brings you no joy at all, stepping back might be right.

If you've given it years of real effort and you've honestly evaluated why it's not working, stepping back might be right.

I'm not telling you to stay in a situation that's killing you. I'm not telling you to sacrifice everything for a dream that isn't worth it.

What I'm telling you is this: Don't walk away because it's hard. Don't walk away because progress is slow. Don't walk away because you got rejected. Don't walk away because you had a bad show.

Those are the wrong reasons. And most wrestlers leave for those reasons.

If you're going to step back, do it because you've genuinely decided wrestling isn't for you. Not because you're tired. Not because you're frustrated. Not because you're scared.

Know the difference.

I Quit. And I Came Back.

I walked away from wrestling in 2002.

I didn't want to. I loved pro wrestling. I loved what I was doing. But my body was breaking down from the injuries. My wife Terrie and I were broke. We were starting a new family. I had to make a choice.

Wrestling or survival.

I chose survival. And I hated it.

Walking away from something you love is one of the hardest things you can do. It felt like a piece of me died. I watched wrestling from the outside, knowing I wasn't part of it anymore. Knowing the guys I came up with were still out there while I was sitting on the sidelines.

But I never stopped paying attention. I kept my finger on the pulse. I watched who was making money. I studied what was working. I stayed connected to the business even when I wasn't in it.

For thirteen years, I was out.

Then in 2015, everything changed.

Terrie and I had accomplished what we set out to do. We'd built a stable life for our family. The kids were in a good place. The finances were solid. And that itch that never went away? It was screaming at me.

I wanted back in.

But I wasn't going back as a full-time wrestler. My body couldn't do that anymore. I needed another way. Starting my own promotion was that way.

New Ohio Wrestling was born because I refused to let walking away be the end of my story. I found a different path back to the thing I loved.

If I could go back and tell my 2002 self anything, it would be this: Focus on your health. And stay in touch with the people you met in the pro wrestling community.

The health part is obvious now. I let myself go for years after I stepped away. I gained weight. I ignored my body. That caught up with me and I'm still dealing with the consequences. If I'd taken care of myself during those thirteen years, I'd be in a much better position today.

The relationships part is just as important. When I came back in 2015, I had to rebuild almost everything from scratch. I did reach out to a core group of guys at the beginning, but the connections I'd made in the early 2000s had faded. People had moved on. If I'd stayed in touch, even just a little, the comeback would have been so much easier.

But here's what matters. I came back. The story wasn't over. Stepping away in 2002 didn't mean stepping away forever.

If you've stepped away from wrestling, you can come back. If you're thinking about walking away, know that the door doesn't have to close permanently. Life has seasons. Sometimes you have to step away. But the dream doesn't have to die.

I'm proof of that.

The Decision That Changes Everything

At some point, you have to decide.

Not "I'll try wrestling and see how it goes." Not "I'll give it a year and evaluate." Not "I'll keep at it unless something better comes along."

A real decision. A commitment. A moment where you say "I'm doing this no matter what."

That decision changes everything.

When you've truly decided, walking away isn't an option. Bad shows don't matter because you're not leaving. Rejection doesn't matter because you're not leaving. Slow progress doesn't matter because you're not leaving.

You just keep going. Because you decided.

The wrestlers who make it have all made this decision. At some point, they stopped wondering if they should continue. They committed. They burned the boats.

Make that decision. Not halfway. Not with an escape hatch. All the way.

Decide that you're not stopping. Then act like it.

Never Quit

The wrestling business will try to make you walk away. It will test you. It will beat you down. It will make you question everything.

Don't.

When the money isn't there, don't stop. Find other ways to make it work.

When progress feels slow, don't stop. Trust the compound curve.

When rejection piles up, don't stop. Keep looking for the right opportunities.

When you have bad shows, don't stop. Learn and come back stronger.

When haters attack you, don't stop. Let them motivate you.

When everyone else gives up, don't stop. Outlast them.

The ones who stay win. The ones who keep showing up get the opportunities. The ones who refuse to walk away build careers.

That's Law #7. Never quit.

Your dream is worth fighting for. Don't let temporary struggles steal permanent success.

Keep going.

CHAPTER 10
LAW #8 – BUILD YOUR TEAM

No wrestler makes it alone.

I know that's not the story we tell. We talk about wrestlers like they're lone wolves. Self-made. Did it all themselves. Rose to the top on pure talent and determination.

That's a lie.

Behind every successful wrestler is a crew. Trainers who taught them. Mentors who guided them. Friends who supported them. Partners who helped them create. Promoters who believed in them. Fans who spread the word.

Nobody makes it alone. Nobody.

The wrestlers who try to do everything themselves burn out. They hit walls they can't break through. They miss opportunities because they don't have the right connections. They stay stuck because they don't have anyone to push them.

The wrestlers who build crews go further. They have people who cover their weaknesses. They have support when things get hard. They have connections that open doors.

Your career depends on the people around you. It's time to build your crew.

The Lone Wolf Myth

The lone wolf thing sounds cool. The wrestler who needs nobody. Who does it all themselves. Who doesn't rely on anyone.

It's sexy. It makes a good story.

It's also stupid.

Lone wolves in nature don't thrive. They survive. Barely. The wolves that thrive are the ones in packs. They hunt together. They protect each other. They're stronger as a group.

Wrestling is the same.

The wrestlers who try to go it alone limit themselves. They can only go as far as their own abilities take them. They can only see what they can see. They can only do what they can do.

The wrestlers who build around themselves multiply what's possible. They have other people's skills, connections, and perspectives. They can go places they couldn't go alone.

Stop trying to be a lone wolf. Start building a pack.

Why You Need a Team

A team covers your weaknesses. You're not good at everything. I know I'm certainly not. Nobody is. You have blind spots. You have skills you lack. You have things you're just not built for. A team fills those gaps. If you're bad at social media, someone on your team can help. If you're weak on promos, someone can coach you. If you don't understand business, someone can guide you. Your weaknesses don't have to hold you back if you have people who are strong where you're weak.

A team opens doors. Opportunities in wrestling come through relationships. Who you know matters. A lot. Every person on your team knows people you don't know. They have connections you don't have. They can introduce you to promoters, wrestlers, and opportunities you'd never find on your own. One introduction from the right person can change your career.

A team keeps you accountable. It's easy to slack off when nobody's watching. It's easy to skip the workout. To not post the content. To not reach out to promoters. When you have a team, people are counting on you. People are checking on you. People notice when you're not doing what you said you'd do. That accountability keeps you moving when motivation fades.

A team supports you when it's hard. Wrestling is brutal. There are times when you'll want to quit. Times when you're broken down. Times when nothing is working. A team picks you up. They remind you why you started. They help you see what you can't see. They carry you when you can't carry yourself. Having people in your corner makes the hard times survivable.

A team makes you better. Iron sharpens iron. When you're around good people, you get better. You learn from them. You're pushed by them. You rise to their level. The people around you shape who you become. Surround yourself with people who make you better and you'll become better.

When No Team Limits a Legend

Ultimate Warrior was one of the most over wrestlers in history.

The energy. The intensity. The entrance that made crowds lose their minds. When Warrior was on, nobody could touch him. He main evented WrestleMania. He beat Hulk Hogan clean. He had the kind of connection with fans that most wrestlers dream about.

But Warrior couldn't keep people around him.

He burned bridges with Vince McMahon. Twice. He burned bridges with WCW. He had public feuds with almost everyone he worked with. Wrestlers who could have been allies became enemies. Promoters who could have made him richer stopped returning his calls. By the end, he'd alienated nearly everyone in the business.

The stories are legendary. Contract disputes that turned ugly. Locker room conflicts that never got resolved. Relationships destroyed over pride and stubbornness. Warrior treated wrestling like a solo act, and the business eventually treated him the same way.

Compare his post-wrestling career to guys like Hulk Hogan or Ric Flair who maintained relationships and kept getting opportunities for decades. Warrior had just as much star power. But he spent years in the wilderness because he'd burned every bridge.

When Warrior finally reconciled with WWE right before his death in 2014, it felt like a miracle. That's how badly he'd damaged his relationships over the years.

All that talent. All that charisma. All that connection with fans. Limited because he couldn't build or keep a circle around him.

Are you building bridges? Or burning them?

Your Inner Circle

Not everyone belongs in your inner circle.

Your inner circle is small. Three to five people max. These are the people closest to your career. The ones you trust completely. The ones who know everything. The ones whose opinions actually matter.

Who belongs in your inner circle?

A trainer or coach. Someone who can teach you. Who can see what you can't see. Who can push you to improve. Who knows the craft and can help you master it. This might be your original trainer. It might be someone you find later. It might be different coaches for different skills. But you need someone in this role.

A mentor. Someone who's been where you want to go. Who's walked the path ahead of you. Who can guide you around the mistakes they made. A mentor isn't necessarily a trainer. They might not teach you skills. But they teach you wisdom. They help you navigate the business. They give you perspective.

A peer. Someone at your level. Who's on the same journey. Who understands what you're going through because they're going through it too. This person keeps you accountable. You push each other. You celebrate wins together. You pick each other up after losses. You're in the trenches together.

A supporter. Someone who believes in you no matter what. Who's in your corner even when things are bad. Who encourages you when you can't encourage yourself. This might be a spouse. A family member. A close friend. Someone who loves you and wants to see you win.

These four roles are your inner circle. You might have one person who fills multiple roles. You might have different people for each. But you need these roles filled.

The Locker Room Is Your Network

A lot of wrestlers miss this: the locker room is a business network.

Every wrestler you work with is a potential connection. They know promoters you don't know. They work for companies you want to work for. They have opportunities they could bring you into.

The relationships you build in locker rooms can make or break your career.

I've seen wrestlers get booked on big shows because someone they worked with put in a good word. I've seen wrestlers get blackballed because they burned bridges with people who ended up in positions of power.

Every interaction in the locker room matters.

Be professional. Be helpful. Be someone people want to work with. Be someone people want to recommend.

You never know who's going to end up where. The green wrestler you're working with today might be booking a major promotion in five years. The guy who seems like a nobody might be connected to someone important.

Treat everyone well. Build relationships with everyone. The locker room is your network.

How to Build Relationships

Building relationships isn't complicated. But most wrestlers don't do it well.

Show up and be professional. This is the baseline. Show up on time. Know your stuff. Work safe. Don't cause drama. Be easy to work with. When you're professional, people notice. They want to work with you again. They recommend you to others.

Help without expecting anything back. Look for ways to help people. Give advice when asked. Share connections. Offer to help with content. Be useful. Don't keep score. Don't help because you want something in return. Help because that's who you are. The people you help will remember. Opportunities will come back to you in ways you didn't expect.

Stay in touch. Relationships die when you don't maintain them. People forget about you if you disappear. Stay in touch with people you've worked with. Not in a pushy way. Just a message here and there. Congratulate them on wins. Share their content. Keep the connection alive. When an opportunity comes up, they'll think of you because you stayed on their radar.

Be genuine. People can smell fake from a mile away. If you're only being nice because you want something, they'll know. Actually care about people. Actually be interested in them. Build real relationships, not transactions. Genuine relationships last. Fake ones crumble when tested.

Finding a Mentor

A mentor can change your career faster than almost anything else.

The right mentor has been where you want to go. They've made mistakes you can avoid. They know things that would take you years to figure out on your own.

One conversation with a great mentor can save you months of struggle.

But mentors don't just appear. You have to find them.

Look for people you respect. Who in wrestling has built what you want to build? Who has the career you're aiming for? Who has the wisdom you need? Make a list. These are potential mentors.

Provide value first. Don't walk up to someone successful and ask them to mentor you. That's backwards. First, provide value. Help them with something. Support their work. Be useful to them. Show that you're serious and worth investing in. Mentorship often grows out of relationships where you've already proven yourself.

Be worth mentoring. Mentors invest in people who will actually use their advice. Who work hard. Who follow through. If you ask for advice and don't take it, mentors stop giving it. If you waste their time, they stop giving you time. Be someone worth mentoring. Do the work. Show results. Make your mentor proud they invested in you.

Ask specific questions. Don't ask a mentor "how do I make it in wrestling?" That's too vague. Ask "How did you approach this situation?" or "What would you do if you were in my position?" or "What's one thing I should focus on right now?" Specific questions get useful answers. Vague questions get vague answers.

Training Partners

Every wrestler needs training partners.

These are the people you drill with. The people you practice promos with. The people you watch videos with. The people who help you get better between shows.

Training alone only gets you so far. You need bodies to work with. You need people to give you feedback. You need the energy of training with others.

Find training partners who take it seriously. Who show up consistently. Who push you to be better.

The best training partners are at your level or slightly better. If they're way below you, you're not getting pushed. If they're way above you, you might not be able to keep up.

Find your people. Train together. Get better together.

Accountability Partners

An accountability partner is someone who keeps you honest.

You tell them what you're going to do. They check in to make sure you did it. They call you out when you're slacking. They celebrate when you follow through.

This sounds simple. It's incredibly powerful.

Most wrestlers have goals they never hit. Things they say they'll do but don't. Plans that fall apart because nobody's watching.

An accountability partner fixes that. When you know someone is going to ask if you did the thing, you're way more likely to do it.

Find someone who's serious about their career too. Someone who wants accountability as much as you do. Hold each other to your commitments.

Check in weekly. Share what you're working on. Report your progress. Be honest when you fall short.

This simple practice will move your career forward faster than almost anything else.

When Rising Together Changes Everything

The Kliq changed wrestling because five guys decided to rise together.

Shawn Michaels. Triple H. Kevin Nash. Scott Hall. Sean Waltman. Five wrestlers who became friends and made a pact: they would look out for each other. They would help each other get ahead.

They would use their individual success to create opportunities for the group.

And it worked.

When one of them had influence, they used it for the others. When one of them got a push, they made sure the others benefited. They shared information. They protected each other politically. They operated as a unit in a business that usually tears people apart.

Look at what they accomplished together. Multiple world championships. Hall of Fame careers. Iconic moments that defined an era. The nWo. D-Generation X. Some of the most important storylines in wrestling history.

What people miss is this: they also built careers that lasted decades after their in-ring days. Triple H runs WWE. Kevin Nash stayed relevant and employed for thirty years. Shawn Michaels became a trainer and producer. They created opportunities for each other long after the matches ended.

None of them would have gone as far alone. Nash has said it. Hall said it. Triple H has said it. The Kliq multiplied what each of them could do individually.

That's the power of a crew. Five guys who decided that rising together beat climbing alone.

Who's in your Kliq? Who are you rising with?

Cutting the Wrong People

Not everyone belongs on your team.

Some people will hold you back. Some people will drain your energy. Some people will sabotage your career.

You need to recognize them and cut them loose.

Energy vampires. People who leave you feeling drained after every interaction. Who complain constantly. Who bring negativity everywhere they go. These people will suck the life out of your career. Distance yourself.

People who don't support your dream. Some people will tell you you're wasting your time. That wrestling is stupid. That you should give up and get a real job. If they're not willing to support your dream, they don't belong in your inner circle.

Users. People who only show up when they need something. Who take and never give. Who see you as a resource to exploit. Real relationships are two-way. If someone only takes, they're not on your team.

Troublemakers. People who cause drama. Who start conflicts. Who burn bridges wherever they go. If you're associated with troublemakers, their reputation affects yours. Stay away.

Cutting people is hard. Especially if you've known them a long time. But your team shapes your career. You can't afford to carry people who are holding you back.

Family

Building a team is essential for a pro wrestling company. I learned that the hard way.

New Ohio Wrestling started as a group of four guys. By the time we really got going, it was down to just me and Terrie. That's how it goes sometimes. People have different visions. Life gets in the way. Partnerships don't always survive.

But it's never really been just me and Terrie. We've had help from tons of people throughout the years, and we value every single one of them.

WrestleFit was built by me and Shawn Jones, but Shawn and Terrie do the actual training for it. I created the concept and became a client. They make it work every day.

The NOW Elite Pro Wrestling Academy is built by Shawn and me together. We both bring the training knowledge. He brings the fitness expertise. I bring the business side and the platform. Neither of us could do it alone.

For New Ohio Wrestling, I've got Peachy Rodriguez and John Orlando helping me with creative and booking. They also help run the back during shows, along with "Papa Smurf" Keith Smith and Ripper Blackhart. We run the back part of the event. Terrie runs the front part of the event. There are so many others who step in and help that if I tried to name them all, I know I'd forget someone.

Something that's changed everything recently: the students at the NOW Elite Pro Wrestling Academy have become a huge part of the crew.

Shawn and I are getting our students trained enough to start wrestling and venture out on their own. But while they're developing, they help in ways that make a massive difference. They fill spots on the card when we need them. They help with setup and teardown. They spread the word about events. They help out during shows with whatever needs doing.

The students and all the others have become our family.

The students even created their own gimmick. At the end of every show, and even some practices, they all stand together with one finger in the air and chant "Family."

No one told them to do that. They created it themselves.

That's how important the students and the training academy are to us. And that's how you know you've built something real. When the people around you feel it so deeply that they create their own traditions. Their own symbols. Their own ways of saying "we're in this together."

That's what a crew becomes when you do it right. It becomes family.

Terrie keeps everything running. Shawn builds the wrestlers. Peachy and John help me book. Keith and Ripper help run the back. The students fill gaps and learn the business. Everyone plays a role.

I couldn't do any of this alone. Nobody can.

Who's on your team? And if you don't have one yet, who do you need to find?

Build Your Team

You can't make it alone. Nobody can.

Build your team.

Find a trainer who can push you. Find a mentor who can guide you. Find peers who can grow with you. Find supporters who believe in you.

Treat the locker room like the business network it is. Build relationships everywhere you go. Help people without expecting anything back.

Find training partners. Get an accountability partner. Rise together with your circle.

Cut the people who hold you back. Keep the people who lift you up.

Your crew will take you places your talent can't reach alone. They'll support you when things get hard. They'll open doors you didn't know existed.

That's Law #8. Build your team.

You weren't meant to do this alone. Stop trying.

CHAPTER 11
LAW #9 – TURN YOUR ANGER INTO FUEL

You're going to get angry.

This business will make sure of it.

You'll get passed over for someone less talented. You'll get stiffed by a promoter who promised to pay you. You'll get talked about behind your back. You'll get rejected for opportunities you deserved. You'll get disrespected by people who don't know half of what you know.

The rage is coming. The question is what you do with it.

Most wrestlers let it destroy them. They explode at the wrong time. They burn bridges. They make enemies. They let bitterness poison their career until there's nothing left.

But some wrestlers do something different. They take that fire and turn it into fuel. They use it to work harder. To perform better. To prove everyone wrong.

Same emotion. Different outcome.

The wrestlers who win are the ones who use their anger instead of letting it use them.

The Power of Negative Emotions

Negative emotions aren't bad. They're powerful.

Frustration. Pain. Resentment. Fear. These emotions carry massive energy. More energy than most positive emotions.

When you're fired up, you have energy to spare. You could run through a wall. You could work all night. You could do things you didn't think you could do.

That energy is a resource. It's fuel waiting to be used.

The problem isn't having negative emotions. The problem is wasting them. Letting them explode in ways that hurt you. Letting them fester until they turn into bitterness. Letting them control you instead of you controlling them.

When you learn to channel negative emotions, you have access to an energy source most people waste. You can outwork people who only run on positive motivation. You can tap into power that makes you dangerous.

Negative emotions aren't your enemy. They're a tool. Learn to use them.

Where the Anger Comes From

Before you can use your anger, you need to understand where it comes from.

In wrestling, it usually comes from a few places.

Disrespect. Someone didn't give you the respect you earned. A promoter treated you like you don't matter. A veteran talked down to you. Someone acted like you don't belong. Disrespect cuts deep. It makes you want to prove them wrong. That's useful energy.

Injustice. You got passed over for someone who didn't deserve it. Politics beat talent. The wrong person got the push. The system screwed you. Injustice creates righteous fury. The feeling that things should be different. That's powerful fuel.

Failure. You messed up. You had a bad match. You botched something important. You didn't perform the way you know you can. Being mad at yourself can be the most powerful kind of fuel. It drives you to fix what's broken. To never let it happen again.

Pain. Physical pain from injuries. Emotional pain from losses. The pain of sacrifice that doesn't seem to pay off. Pain creates a burning desire to make it worth something. To not let the suffering be for nothing.

Doubt. People who said you couldn't do it. The voice in your head that says you're not good enough. The fear that maybe they're right. The fire that comes from doubt is the fire of proving everyone wrong. Including yourself.

All of these are sources of fuel. The question is whether you'll use them or let them use you.

The Bad Guy Advantage

Heels have an advantage when it comes to using negative energy.

A heel's job is to channel dark emotions. To be resentful. To want to hurt people. To act on what's boiling inside.

When a heel is genuinely fired up, it makes their performance better. The emotion is real. The intensity is real. The crowd feels it.

A babyface has to channel positive emotions. Hope. Heart. Fighting spirit. That's harder to do when you're actually furious about something in real life.

This is the bad guy advantage. Heels can use their real negative emotions in their performance. They can take what's bothering them and put it in the ring.

If you're working heel, use this. Take your real frustrations and channel them through your character. Let your actual fire fuel your promos and your matches.

The best heels aren't acting. They're channeling. They're taking real emotions and pointing them in a useful direction.

Using Anger as Workout Fuel

One of the best places to channel that fire is in training.

When you're heated, you have extra energy. Extra intensity. Extra drive. Use it.

Had a bad day? Hit the gym harder than usual. Got rejected by a promoter? Take it out on the weights. Someone disrespected you? Run until you can't run anymore.

Physical training is the perfect outlet. You burn off the negative energy. You get stronger. You turn something destructive into something constructive.

I've had some of my best workouts when I was furious. The emotion gave me fuel I didn't normally have. I lifted more. I pushed harder. I did things I couldn't do on a normal day.

Next time you're heated, don't sit with it. Don't vent on social media. Don't start drama. Go train.

Turn the fire into muscle. Turn the frustration into cardio. Turn the pain into strength.

Using Anger as Performance Fuel

That same fire can fuel your performance.

Some wrestlers perform better when they're heated. They're more intense. More focused. More believable. The emotion comes through in everything they do.

I've seen wrestlers have the match of their life because they were carrying something heavy into the ring. The emotion gave them an edge. Made them sharper. Made them care more.

If you're about to perform and you're carrying frustration, don't try to push it down. Use it.

Channel it into your character. Let it fuel your intensity. Let it make your strikes stiffer, your facials more real, your promos more passionate.

The crowd doesn't know why you're fired up. They just feel that something's different. That you mean it more than usual. That this matters.

On many occasions, I would take my frustrations into the ring with me and use them. Not only did it help my performance, it let me blow off some steam and release that tension. I would go to the ring in a terrible mood and come back smiling and less stressed because I left it all in the ring.

Using Anger as Creative Fuel

That fire can also drive creativity.

Some of the best promos, characters, and storylines come from real frustration. Wrestlers who were furious about how they were being used. Mad about not getting opportunities. Fed up with the business.

They channeled those emotions into their creative work. They wrote promos that dripped with real resentment. They created characters that embodied their frustrations. They pitched ideas that came from a genuine place.

Some of the most memorable promos in wrestling history came from wrestlers who were genuinely frustrated. Who had real things they wanted to say. Who channeled real fire into their words.

When you're mad about something in your career, ask yourself:

- Is there creative work here?
- Can this frustration become a promo?
- Can this pain become a character element?
- Can this resentment become content?

That kind of emotion wants to be expressed. Creative work is one of the healthiest ways to express it.

When Anger Becomes Legend

Steve Austin turned real fury into the biggest character in wrestling history.

Before Stone Cold, Austin was "Stunning" Steve Austin in WCW. Bleach blonde. Pretty boy. Tag team wrestler. He was good, but he wasn't special. And WCW treated him that way.

Then Eric Bischoff fired him over the phone while he was injured. Didn't even have the respect to do it in person.

Austin was furious. And he used every ounce of that fury.

When he got to WWE, he channeled all that resentment, all that "I'll show you" energy into creating Stone Cold Steve Austin. The bald head. The black trunks. The middle fingers. The beer. The attitude.

Stone Cold wasn't acting. He was channeling. All the frustration from being overlooked in WCW. All the rage at being fired like he didn't matter. All the years of feeling disrespected. He poured it all into a character that felt more real than anything wrestling had ever seen.

The Austin 3:16 promo? That was real fire coming through. The beer bashing? Real resentment at authority. The stunners to Vince McMahon? Real frustration at every boss who ever held him back.

And it worked. Stone Cold Steve Austin became the biggest star in wrestling. He main evented WrestleMania. He drew more money than almost anyone in history. He changed the entire business.

All because he took his fury and turned it into fuel instead of letting it destroy him.

Eric Bischoff firing him over the phone might have been the best thing that ever happened to Steve Austin. Because it gave him the fire he needed to become a legend.

What are you doing with your anger?

Using Anger to Prove Them Wrong

One of the most powerful uses of that fire: proving them wrong.

Someone said you couldn't do it? Prove them wrong.

Someone passed you over? Prove them wrong.

Someone counted you out? Prove them wrong.

This is revenge through success. Instead of getting mad and doing something stupid, you get mad and do something great.

Every time you succeed, it's a middle finger to everyone who doubted you. Every win is proof they were wrong. Every milestone is evidence that you belong.

This kind of fuel is sustainable. It doesn't burn out because there's always someone new to prove wrong. It doesn't require you to do anything destructive. It just requires you to succeed.

Some of the most successful people in any field are driven by this. The chip on their shoulder. The list of people who doubted them. The burning desire to make everyone eat their words.

Keep a list if you have to. Remember who said you couldn't. Remember who passed you over. Remember who disrespected you.

Then go prove them all wrong.

The Danger of Uncontrolled Anger

Now the dark side.

Uncontrolled anger is destructive.

I've seen wrestlers destroy their careers in moments of rage. Said the wrong thing to the wrong person. Burned a bridge they needed. Made an enemy they couldn't afford.

I've seen wrestlers let bitterness consume them. They became so bitter about the business that they couldn't enjoy anything. Every conversation became a complaint. Every interaction became negative. Nobody wanted to be around them.

I've seen wrestlers let it affect their work. They got stiff with opponents they were mad at. They no-showed because they were upset. They sabotaged themselves because they couldn't control their emotions.

Uncontrolled emotion will ruin you.

The goal isn't to be fired up all the time. The goal isn't to let rage run your life. The goal is to use it when it shows up, then let it go.

Feel it. Use it. Release it.

Don't hold onto it. Don't let it fester. Don't let it turn into bitterness.

Anger is a temporary fuel source. Use it while it's there, then move on.

When Anger Destroys Everything

New Jack let rage run his life. And it destroyed him.

Watch his matches. The guy was intense. He had a connection with crowds that was undeniable. When his music hit and he came out with that garbage can full of weapons, people went crazy. He was a legitimate draw in ECW during its peak.

But New Jack couldn't control himself.

The stories are legendary. And not in a good way. He stabbed a wrestler in the ring during a match. Multiple times. He threw a man off a scaffold and nearly killed him. He openly talked about wanting to hurt people for real. He had legitimate violent incidents that went far beyond working.

His rage wasn't a character. It was who he was. And it made him dangerous to work with.

Promoters stopped booking him because the liability was too high. Wrestlers refused to work with him because they didn't trust him.

His reputation became so toxic that despite his drawing ability, nobody wanted the risk.

New Jack blamed everyone else. The business. The promoters. The wrestlers who "couldn't handle" him. But the truth was simpler. He couldn't control his emotions, and it made him unemployable.

He could have been remembered as an ECW legend who helped define hardcore wrestling. Instead, he's remembered as a cautionary tale about what happens when your emotions control you instead of you controlling them.

Talent means nothing if nobody will work with you. Drawing ability means nothing if you're too dangerous to book.

Are you controlling your emotions? Or are they controlling you?

Control Your Emotions or They Control You

You have to be in control.

Anger is a tool. Tools are meant to be used by you, not the other way around. If it's making your decisions, if it's running your life, you've lost control.

The difference between successful people and unsuccessful people isn't whether they feel negative emotions. Everyone does. The difference is whether they control those emotions or get controlled by them.

When you're in control, you choose when to use the energy. You choose where to direct it. You choose when to let it go. The emotion serves you.

When you're not in control, it uses you. It explodes at the wrong time. It directs itself at the wrong targets. It lingers long after it should have faded. The emotion runs you.

This is a skill. It takes practice. It takes self-awareness. It takes work.

But it's one of the most important skills you can develop. The ability to feel powerful emotions without being controlled by them. The ability to use your fire instead of being used by it.

Master this and you have an advantage most people don't have.

Other Negative Emotions

Anger isn't the only negative emotion you can use.

Frustration can drive persistence. When something isn't working, frustration makes you want to figure it out. To try harder. To NOT give up until you crack it.

Fear can drive preparation. When you're scared of failing, you prepare more. You train harder. You make sure you're ready.

Pain can drive empathy. When you've suffered, you understand others who are suffering. That understanding can make you a better performer, a better leader, a better person.

Sadness can drive depth. Some of the most moving performances come from wrestlers channeling real sadness. Real loss. Real grief.

Doubt can drive humility. When you're not sure if you're good enough, you stay hungry. You keep working. You don't get complacent.

All negative emotions carry energy. All of them can be channeled. The question is always the same: Will you use them or will they use you?

When to Let It Go

Not every battle is worth fighting.

Some things that make you furious aren't worth your energy. Some people who disrespect you don't matter. Some injustices are too small to carry around.

Part of using anger well is knowing when to let it go.

If the frustration is about something that doesn't affect your mission, let it go. If it's about someone whose opinion doesn't matter, let it go. If it's served its purpose and there's nothing more to gain from it, let it go.

Carrying rage that serves no purpose is just weight. It slows you down. It takes up space in your head. It drains energy you could use for something else.

Use it when it's useful. Let it go when it's not.

The ability to release anger is just as important as the ability to channel it.

How Anger Almost Cost Me Everything

For the most part, it's the little stuff that gets me fired up.

If a big problem comes along, I can usually step up to the plate and find a solution. I stay calm. I figure it out. I handle it.

But the little stuff? The things that are easily fixable? The problems that shouldn't even be problems? That's what gets me riled up. Because it didn't have to happen. Because someone didn't do what they were supposed to do. Because a simple situation became complicated for no reason.

But sometimes you have to let it go. Even when you think you're right.

This is how anger almost cost me the Arnold Sports Festival.

My first show with New Ohio Wrestling was at a soccer facility. The show itself was great but dealing with the facility went bad. Silly disagreements between the owner and me. Things that could have been easily avoided. The whole experience left a bad taste in my mouth.

I made a decision after that. I would never work with a soccer facility again. Done. Off the list. Not happening.

That bitterness sat with me for years.

Later, I was looking for a facility to run an event. Someone gave me a tip about a new soccer facility opening up close by.

My first reaction? No way. I'm not doing that again. I'm not dealing with soccer facility owners. I learned my lesson.

But something made me check it out anyway. Maybe I was desperate. Maybe I was curious. Maybe I was just willing to give it a shot despite the grudge.

What I found was totally unexpected.

The owners were incredibly nice. They were willing to work with me. They understood what I was trying to do. And here's where it gets crazy.

They had friends in high places. They themselves were part of the Arnold SportsWorld Kids & Teens Expo. They knew people. They had connections.

They vouched for me. They helped me get my start with the Arnold.

If I had stayed bitter at soccer facilities in general and never approached them, there is a great chance I would have never gotten into the Arnold Sports Festival.

Let that sink in.

The Arnold. The biggest multi-sport festival in the world. The thing that put New Ohio Wrestling on the map. The achievement nobody can take away from us.

I almost missed it because I was holding onto a grudge from years earlier.

Anger is fuel. Use it. But know when to let it go.

If I'd let that old bitterness make my decisions, I would have driven right past the opportunity of a lifetime. Instead, I checked my emotions at the door, gave someone new a chance, and it changed everything.

Feel it. Use it. Release it.

That's the formula.

Turn Your Anger Into Fuel

You're going to feel fired up. This business guarantees it.

The question is what you do with it.

You can let rage explode and destroy your career. You can let bitterness eat you alive. You can let your emotions control your decisions and your behavior.

Or you can use it.

Channel it into your training. Channel it into your performance. Channel it into your creative work. Channel it into proving everyone wrong.

Feel it. Use it. Release it.

Control your emotions or they'll control you. Master your fire or it'll master you.

That's Law #9. Turn your anger into fuel.

The same energy that destroys other people can be the energy that builds your career. It all depends on what you do with it.

Use it wisely.

CHAPTER 12
LAW #10 – TRAIN YOUR BRAIN

You train your body every week.

You hit the gym. You drill moves. You work on your cardio. You take bumps. You practice promos. You put in the physical work.

But do you train your brain?

Most wrestlers don't. They spend hours on their body and zero time on their mind. They think mental training is soft. Unnecessary. Something for people who aren't tough enough.

That's backwards.

Your mind controls everything. How you perform under pressure. How you handle rejection. How you bounce back from failure. How you see yourself. How confident you feel in the ring.

A wrestler with a trained body and an untrained mind will always lose to a wrestler who has trained both.

Your mind is either your biggest weapon or your biggest enemy. It's time to make sure it's a weapon.

The Voice in Your Head

There's a voice in your head.

It talks to you all day long. It comments on everything you do. It judges you. It predicts the future. It reminds you of the past.

Sometimes that voice helps you. It encourages you. It tells you that you can do this. It reminds you of your wins.

Sometimes that voice destroys you. It tells you you're not good enough. It reminds you of every failure. It predicts disaster before you even try.

That voice shapes your reality. What it says becomes what you believe. What you believe becomes how you act. How you act becomes what you achieve.

If the voice in your head is constantly negative, you're fighting an uphill battle every single day. You're carrying weight that other people don't carry. You're beating yourself before anyone else gets the chance.

If the voice in your head is positive and supportive, everything gets easier. You move through the world with confidence. You bounce back faster. You perform at your best.

The voice isn't fixed. You can change it. You can train it. That's what mental training is.

Your Brain Believes What You Tell It

Your mind believes what you tell it.

If you tell yourself you're a loser, your mind believes it. It looks for evidence to support that belief. It filters out evidence that contradicts it. It makes the belief feel true even if it isn't.

If you tell yourself you're a winner, your mind believes that too. It looks for evidence that you're a winner. It filters out the stuff that doesn't fit. It makes winning feel natural and expected.

Same brain. Different programming. Completely different results.

This isn't wishful thinking. This is how the brain actually works. It's called confirmation bias. Your mind finds what it's looking for. It creates the reality that matches what you believe.

So what are you telling yourself?

What do you say when you mess up? What do you think before a big match? What do you believe about your future?

Those thoughts are programming your mind. They're shaping what you see, what you believe, and what you achieve.

If you want different results, you need different programming.

The Problem With Negative Self-Talk

Most wrestlers are brutal to themselves.

They say things to themselves they'd never say to a friend. They beat themselves up for every mistake. They replay failures over and over. They predict disaster constantly.

"I'm going to mess this up."

"I'm not as good as them."

"They're going to see I don't belong."

"That was terrible. I'm terrible."

"I'll never make it."

This is negative self-talk. And it's poison.

Every time you say something negative to yourself, you're programming your mind. You're strengthening the neural pathways that support that belief. You're making it more likely you'll think the same thing next time.

Over time, negative self-talk becomes automatic. It becomes the default voice in your head. It becomes so normal you don't even notice it anymore.

But your performance notices. Your confidence notices. Your career notices.

Negative self-talk is sabotage. You're sabotaging yourself from the inside. No opponent can do as much damage to you as your own mind when it's working against you.

When an Untrained Brain Betrays You

Sid Vicious had everything you could want physically.

Six foot nine. Jacked. Imposing. When he walked to the ring, he looked like the final boss of wrestling. He had the presence that most wrestlers would kill for. He main evented WrestleMania. Twice. He held world championships in both WWE and WCW.

But Sid's mind was his biggest enemy.

The promo disasters are legendary. "I have half the brain that you do." The moments where he'd lose his train of thought mid-sentence. The times where you could see him mentally checking out in the middle of a match.

Sid was notorious for getting in his own head. He'd have mental lapses at the worst possible moments. He'd lose focus when the pressure was highest. He'd make mistakes that someone with his experience shouldn't make.

The scariest example happened at WCW Sin 2001. Sid went for a big boot off the second rope, landed wrong, and snapped his leg in half on live television. One of the most gruesome injuries in wrestling history. Now, injuries happen. But people who worked with Sid talked about how he wasn't mentally present that night. How he seemed off. How the mental lapses had been building.

Compare Sid to guys who were smaller, less impressive physically, but who had bulletproof mental games. They lasted longer. They performed more consistently. They reached heights Sid never sustained.

Sid had every physical tool. But he never trained the tool that mattered most. His mind worked against him his entire career. And it showed at the worst possible times.

Your body can be a weapon. But if your mind isn't trained, it will sabotage everything your body can do.

Are you training your mind? Or just your body?

Rewiring Your Brain

The good news is you can change it.

Your brain can change. It can be rewired. The pathways that support negative thinking can be weakened. New pathways that support positive thinking can be built.

But it takes work. It takes repetition. It takes conscious effort over time.

You didn't develop negative self-talk overnight. You won't fix it overnight either. But you can fix it.

The process is simple. Not easy, but simple.

First, you have to notice the negative thoughts. You have to catch yourself when you're being brutal to yourself. Most people don't even notice because it's so automatic.

Second, you have to interrupt the pattern. When you notice a negative thought, you stop it. You don't let it run. You don't let it spiral.

Third, you have to replace it with something better. Not fake positivity. Not lies. Something true and helpful.

"I'm going to mess this up" becomes "I've prepared for this. I can handle it."

"I'm not as good as them" becomes "I have my own strengths. I belong here."

"That was terrible" becomes "That wasn't my best. I'll learn and do better next time."

This feels awkward at first. Fake. Forced. But over time, the new thoughts become more natural. The new pathways get stronger. The old pathways get weaker.

You're literally rewiring your brain. Thought by thought. Day by day.

Affirmations for Wrestlers

Affirmations are statements you repeat to yourself to program your mind.

Some people think affirmations are cheesy. Standing in front of a mirror saying nice things to yourself. It feels silly.

But affirmations work. Not because they're magic. Because repetition changes the brain.

The key is using affirmations that actually mean something to you. Not generic feel-good stuff. Statements that connect to your mission, your identity, your goals.

Examples of affirmations that work for wrestlers:

"I belong in this ring."

"I am a professional. I show up and deliver every time."

"My best performances are ahead of me."

"I get better every single day."

"I am the hardest worker in the room."

"I handle pressure with confidence."

"I deserve success and I'm building it."

"Every setback makes me stronger."

"I control what I can control and release the rest."

"I am becoming the wrestler I want to be."

Pick a few that resonate with you. Say them every morning. Say them before matches. Say them when you're struggling.

At first it feels weird. Over time it becomes powerful. Your mind starts to believe what you're telling it. Your actions start to match your beliefs.

Here's the thing about affirmations. Reading examples in a book isn't enough.

You have to actually do them. Every day. Consistently. Over time. That's how the brain changes. Not by understanding the concept but by putting in the daily reps.

I built a free 30-Day Mindset Challenge to make sure you actually do the work. Every day for 30 days you get a specific mental training task. Affirmations. Visualization. Self-talk exercises. Pressure handling drills. The same kind of daily mental reps that John Cena was putting in while everyone else was just training their bodies.

Thirty days of consistent work won't fix everything. But it will change something. And something is how it starts.

Download it free at **prowrestlingskool.com**

Then come back. Because the next section covers what to do with your mind right before you walk through that curtain.

Pre-Match Mental Routines

The best wrestlers have mental routines they do before every match.

Not just physical warm-ups. Mental preparation. Getting their mind in the right state to perform.

This matters because your mental state affects your performance. If you're anxious, scattered, and full of doubt, you'll perform worse. If you're calm, focused, and confident, you'll perform better.

A pre-match mental routine puts you in the right state on purpose. Instead of leaving your mental state to chance, you take control of it.

Breathing. Deep, slow breaths calm your nervous system. They take you out of fight-or-flight mode and into a state where you can perform. A few minutes of intentional breathing can completely change how you feel.

Visualization. See yourself performing well. Run through the match in your mind. See yourself hitting your spots, connecting with the crowd, getting the reactions you want. Make it vivid. Make it real.

Affirmations. Repeat a few key statements to yourself. Remind yourself who you are and what you're capable of. Program your mind for success right before you need it.

Focus cues. Pick one or two things to focus on during the match. Not everything. Just a couple key things. This gives your mind something to lock onto instead of spiraling into anxiety.

Physical triggers. Some wrestlers have physical actions that put them in the zone. Slapping themselves. Jumping up and down. A specific stretch. Something that signals to the body that it's time to perform.

Build a routine that works for you. Do it before every match. Make it automatic. Your mind will learn to associate the routine with performance state. Eventually, the routine itself will trigger confidence.

Post-Match Mental Recovery

What you do after a match matters too.

Most wrestlers either ignore what happened or beat themselves up about mistakes. Neither is helpful.

Good mental recovery has a structure.

Acknowledge what went well. Even in a bad match, something went right. Find it. Acknowledge it. Let your mind register the wins.

Identify what to improve. Not from a place of shame. From a place of growth. What can you learn? What would you do differently? What will you work on?

Release the rest. Once you've extracted the lessons, let the match go. Don't replay it endlessly. Don't beat yourself up. It's over. The only thing that matters now is the next one.

This process trains your mind to handle matches in a healthy way. You learn without getting destroyed by mistakes. You improve without getting arrogant about successes.

The wrestlers who do this recover faster emotionally. They don't carry bad matches around for weeks. They learn and move on.

Handling Pressure

Pressure makes some wrestlers shine. It makes others crumble.

The difference isn't talent. It's mental training.

When you understand pressure, you can handle it better.

Pressure is just importance plus uncertainty. You feel pressure when something matters and you're not sure how it's going to go.

You can't always reduce the importance. Big matches matter. Important moments matter. That's not going to change.

But you can reduce the uncertainty. The more prepared you are, the less uncertain you feel. The more you've visualized success, the more certain your mind feels. The more you trust yourself, the less pressure gets to you.

You can also reframe pressure. Instead of "this is scary and I might fail," you can think "this is exciting and I get to show what I can do."

The physical sensations of pressure and excitement are almost identical. Racing heart. Butterflies in your stomach. Heightened awareness. Your mind decides whether that's fear or excitement.

Train yourself to interpret pressure as excitement. As opportunity. As a chance to perform.

The wrestlers who thrive under pressure aren't fearless. They've just trained their minds to respond differently.

When a Trained Brain Makes a Legend

John Cena's mental game might be the strongest in wrestling history.

Consider what he dealt with. Half the audience booing him every night for over a decade. "Cena sucks" chants during his biggest moments. Internet fans calling him the worst thing to happen to wrestling. Constant criticism of his work, his character, his push.

Most wrestlers would crumble under that. Most wrestlers would doubt themselves. Most wrestlers would let it affect their performance.

Cena never did.

He walked to that ring with the same energy whether the crowd was cheering or booing. He delivered in the main event of WrestleMania like the pressure didn't exist. He cut promos with confidence when thousands of people were telling him he sucked. He showed up, night after night, year after year, with the same unshakeable belief in himself.

That's not natural. That's trained.

Cena has talked about his mental preparation. The visualization. The focus. The ability to block out the noise and lock in on what matters. He didn't let the external chaos become internal chaos. He controlled what he could control and released the rest.

The result? One of the greatest careers in wrestling history. Seventeen world championships. Main events for two decades. A successful transition to Hollywood. A legacy that will last forever.

John Cena wasn't the most technically gifted wrestler. He wasn't the best worker. But his mental game was so strong that it didn't matter. He could access his full ability when it mattered most. He performed under pressure better than almost anyone.

That's what a trained mind looks like.

What would your career look like if your mental game was bulletproof?

Fixing Limiting Beliefs

Limiting beliefs are deep thoughts that hold you back.

They're different from everyday negative self-talk. They're bigger. More fundamental. They shape how you see yourself and what you think is possible.

Examples of limiting beliefs:

"I'm not the kind of person who succeeds."

"People like me don't make it in wrestling."

"I don't have what it takes."

"I'll never be as good as them."

"Success isn't for people from my background."

"I'm just not a confident person."

These beliefs feel like facts. They feel like the truth about who you are. But they're not facts. They're stories you've told yourself so many times that they feel true.

Limiting beliefs are sneaky. They work in the background. You might not even know you have them. But they affect everything.

If you believe you're not the kind of person who succeeds, you'll sabotage yourself whenever you get close to success. If you believe you don't have what it takes, you won't put in full effort because what's the point?

Finding and fixing limiting beliefs is some of the most important mental work you can do. It requires honesty. It requires looking at patterns in your life. It requires asking why you keep getting the same results.

What do you believe about yourself at the deepest level? Is it true? Is it serving you?

If not, it's time to change the story.

The Long Game of Mental Training

Mental training isn't a one-time thing.

You don't do it once and you're fixed. You do it every day. You build the habits. You put in the reps. Just like physical training.

Some days will be harder than others. Some days the negative voice will be louder. Some days you'll slip back into old patterns.

That's normal. It's not failure. It's part of the process.

What matters is that you keep going. You keep catching the negative thoughts. You keep replacing them. You keep doing your routines. You keep building the muscle.

Over time, the changes stick. The positive voice gets stronger. The negative voice gets weaker. The routines become automatic. Your mind becomes a weapon instead of an enemy.

It takes months to see real change. Years to fully transform your mental game. But every day you train your mind, you're getting stronger.

The wrestlers who commit to this have an advantage that compounds over time. Their mental game gets better and better. They handle pressure better. They bounce back faster. They perform more consistently.

Mental training is the edge that most wrestlers ignore. That makes it an opportunity for you.

My Battle With Imposter Syndrome

Most of my life I've struggled with imposter syndrome.

Even as a kid, I would get into my own head. Am I good enough? Who do I think I am? What makes me think I can do this? That voice followed me everywhere. Into school. Into work. Into wrestling.

When I was actively wrestling, I didn't know what mental training was. I just pushed through. I ignored the voice and hoped it would go away. It didn't.

It wasn't until after I had to leave pro wrestling that I discovered mental training.

I started listening to Tony Robbins seminars. I started reading books by Napoleon Hill, Elsie Lincoln Benedict, Dale Carnegie, Earl Nightingale, and Jim Rohn. These people opened my eyes to how the mind actually works. How the voice in your head can be changed. How your beliefs shape your reality.

I also started studying business training. Russell Brunson. Dan Kennedy. Dean Graziosi. Alex Hormozi. Gary Vaynerchuk. Perry Belcher. Frank Kern. And many others. Learning how to market and build businesses also taught me how to build my mindset.

Studying all of these brilliant people is how I learned the stuff I'm writing about in this book.

Everything you've read so far? The laws of success? The mental frameworks? The business strategies? I didn't make this up. I learned it from people who figured it out before me. I took their wisdom and applied it to pro wrestling.

The irony? Writing this book is helping me with my imposter syndrome.

That voice still shows up. Who do you think you are to write a book? What makes you qualified to teach this stuff? Who's going to listen to you?

But I've trained my mind to respond differently now.

I know that imposter syndrome is just a sign that I'm stretching. That I'm doing something that matters. That I'm stepping outside my comfort zone.

I know that the voice isn't telling the truth. It's just scared. And I don't let scared voices make my decisions anymore.

Studying these mentors gave me the confidence to spread my message to the world. To talk about the mental and business aspects of pro wrestling that nobody else is teaching. To build Pro Wrestling Skool and write this book and create something that helps wrestlers change their lives.

The voice still talks. I just don't let it win anymore.

That's what mental training does. It doesn't make the voice disappear. It teaches you how to respond to it. It gives you tools to override the doubt and take action anyway.

If you struggle with imposter syndrome, with self-doubt, with that voice that tells you you're not good enough, you're not alone. I've dealt with it my whole life.

But you can train your mind. You can learn to respond differently. You can build the mental game that lets you perform at your best.

Start with the books. Start with the seminars. Start with the work.

Your mind is trainable. Train it.

Train Your Brain

Your mind is either working for you or against you. There's no neutral.

If you don't train it, it will default to negativity. It will beat you up. It will hold you back. It will sabotage you at the worst possible moments.

If you do train it, it becomes your greatest asset. It supports you. It drives you. It helps you perform at your best when it matters most.

Train your mind like you train your body. Every day. With intention. With consistency.

Watch your self-talk. Use affirmations. Build pre-match routines. Practice post-match recovery. Learn to handle pressure. Find and fix your limiting beliefs.

This is the work that most wrestlers won't do. Which is exactly why you should do it.

That's Law #10. Train your brain.

Your mind is the most powerful tool you have. Make sure it's working for you.

WHAT COMES NEXT

You made it through the foundation.

You know your wrestler type. You understand how your brain works. You know where your strengths live and where your blind spots hide.

You learned the 10 Laws that separate the wrestlers who make it from the ones who fade out. Mission. Belief. Skill. Imagination. Planning. Decisions. Persistence. Team. Anger. Mental training.

That's more than most wrestlers will ever learn about building a career.

But here's the truth. Knowing yourself and training your mind is only half the game.

The other half is people and money.

You can have the strongest mindset in the locker room and still go broke if you don't understand the business side. You can believe in yourself completely and still sit at home waiting for the phone to ring if you don't know how to read promoters. You can have a perfect plan and still stay invisible if you don't know how to build a brand.

That's what Book Two covers. Pro Wrestling Laws of Business takes over where the Pro Wrestling Laws of Success left off.

Reading People. How to understand promoters and give them what they need. How to work a crowd so they care about you. How to read your opponent and have a great match with anyone. How to make a first impression that sticks.

Building Your Business. How to think like an owner instead of an employee. How to create multiple income streams so you're never one bad booking away from broke. How to build your brand outside the ring. How to create digital products, communities, and systems that pay you whether you're wrestling or not.

Your Legacy. How to build real freedom. How to become a leader in the locker room. How to think 10 and 20 years ahead. How to build something that outlasts your body's ability to take bumps.

The 10 Laws you just learned are the engine. Pro Wrestling Laws of Business shows you where to drive it.

JOIN THE COMMUNITY

While you wait for Book Two, come join us inside Pro Wrestling Skool. It's a free online community where wrestlers learn how to build brands, grow audiences, and make real money. You'll get access to the tools that go with this book. The 3R Framework on one page. A 30-day mindset challenge. Weekly planning templates. A gimmick development worksheet. A content calendar. And a growing library of resources to keep you moving forward.

The book gives you the laws. The community gives you the tools to put them to work.

Come join us. The door is open.

I'll see you inside.

www.prowrestlingskool.com

— Donnie Hoover

ABOUT THE AUTHOR

Donnie Hoover is a semi-retired professional wrestler, promoter, trainer, gym owner, and digital entrepreneur. He has been in and around the professional wrestling business since 1997.

He is the founder of New Ohio Wrestling, a family-friendly live wrestling promotion. He owns and operates NOW Elite Pro Wrestling Academy, where he trains the next generation of professional wrestlers. He runs WrestleFit Training & Lifestyle Center, a pro-wrestling-inspired functional fitness gym. And he built Pro Wrestling Skool, a global online education platform teaching wrestlers how to build brands, create content, and make money.

Donnie created the 3R Framework (Reach, Reputation, Revenue) as the foundation for everything he teaches. His mission is to build the first real business education system for the professional wrestling industry.

The Pro Wrestling Laws of Success is Book One of The Pro Wrestling Laws Trilogy. It teaches the mental game that makes everything else possible.

Donnie lives in Ohio with his wife Terrie. When he's not building businesses or training wrestlers, he's watching slasher films. Jason Voorhees is the GOAT.

Connect with Donnie

www.ProWrestlingSkool.com
New Ohio Wrestling
NOW Elite Pro Wrestling Academy
WrestleFit Training & Lifestyle Center
Pro Wrestling Skool

ACKNOWLEDGMENTS

This book wouldn't exist without the people who believed in it before it was finished.

To Terrie. You've stood next to me through every crazy idea, every late night, and every time the bank account said we should quit. You never did. This book exists because you believed in it before anyone else.

To my students at NOW Elite Pro Wrestling Academy. You're the reason I keep teaching. Every question you ask makes me better at explaining this stuff. This book is for you.

To the New Ohio Wrestling roster and crew. You show up every event and put on a show. You remind me why I fell in love with this business in the first place.

To the Pro Wrestling Skool community. You took a chance on something new. You trusted me to build something worth your time. I don't take that lightly.

And to the wrestling business itself. It gave me bumps, bruises, bad hot dogs, empty arenas, canceled shows, and the best education money can't buy. I wouldn't trade a single mile.

ONE MORE THING

If this book helped you, please leave a review.

Your review helps other wrestlers find this book and change their careers.

And if you know a wrestler who needs to read this, send them a copy.

The wrestling business gets better when we lift each other up.

www.ingramcontent.com/pod-product-compliance
Lightning Source LLC
LaVergne TN
LVHW010616100826
845148LV00014B/2989

9780983067733